# Red Tory Red Virgin

### Essays on Simone Weil and George P. Grant

### Brad Jersak

RED TORY, RED VIRGIN
Essays on Simone Weil and George P. Grant
Copyright © 2012 by Brad Jersak

All rights reserved. No part of this publication may be reproduced, stored in a retrieval system, or transmitted in any form or by any means—electronic, mechanical, photocopy, recording, or any other—except for brief quotations in printed reviews, without the prior written permission of the author. For further information, contact Fresh Wind Press at freshwind@shaw.ca

Printed through www.createspace.com
To contact the author: freshwind@shaw.ca

ISBN: 978-1-927512-00-5
ebook ISBN: 978-1-927512-01-2

Library and Archives Canada Cataloguing in Publication

Jersak, Brad, 1964-
    Red Tory, Red Virgin : essays on Simone Weil and George P. Grant / by Brad Jersak.

Includes bibliographical references.

    1. Grant, George, 1918-1988. 2. Grant, George, 1918-1988--Criticism and interpretation. 3. Grant, George, 1918-1988--Contemporaries. I. Jersak, Brad, 1964 II. Title.

Fresh Wind Press
2170 Maywood Ct.,
Abbotsford, BC
Canada V2S 4Z1
www.freshwindpress.com

# Red Tory Red Virgin

Essays on Simone Weil
and George P. Grant

Brad Jersak

**For Simone Weil**

"... her thought is, next to the Gospels,
the highest authority for me."

—G. Grant

# Table of Contents

Preface / 1

### Part 1 – SIMONE WEIL: RED VIRGIN

1. Simone Weil: George Grant's Diotima / 5
2. Stages of Weil's Mystical Ascent / 19
3. Competing Conceptions of God in Biblical Religion / 49

### Part 2 – GEORGE GRANT: RED TORY

4. Grant and the Matrix: Complex of Ideologies / 71
5. Grant and the Matrix: Dialogue Partners / 75
6. Finding His Voice: Conversion to *Lament* / 83

### Part 3 – DIVINE CONSENT

7. Wrath and Love as Divine Consent / 109

Abbreviations / 123

Bibliography of Sources Consulted / 127

# Preface

I do not know what it is like for those who learn about Simone Weil in a classroom or study her from a textbook. I don't know how her life and writings would seem to the casual peruser or the objective scholar. I imagine she would seem odd and extreme, someone from who to glean a few 'tweetable' aphorisms before moving on.

In my case, it felt more like it was Weil who discovered me—one who breathed words of life into my drowning spirit before I went under for the last time. Sparing the reader the gory details, I will simply testify to the lifesaving impact of her famous statement, *"I am ceaselessly torn between the perfection of God and the misery of man."*

Through that confession, Weil gave me permission to stand in simultaneous astonishment before the goodness of God and the affliction of humanity, admitting the real contradiction between the two. She led me to gaze into the abyss, where she called me to behold the mystery of the Cross of Christ, the universal intersection and golden balance of divine love and human suffering.

As best as I understand him, George Grant, Canada's great Red Tory, experienced Weil, the infamous 'Red Virgin,' in a remarkably similar way. He was convinced of her authority and inspiration as a genuine saint for cruciform justice.

In this work of essays, I continue the explorations on Grant and Weil begun in two previous works, *GPG: Canada's Lone Wolf* (2011, with Ron Dart) and *GPG: Minerva's Snowy Owl* (2012). These three works form a trilogy of research that interdepends as primary and supplementary research alongside my PhD thesis (Bangor University, Wales), *"We are not our own: the Platonic Christianity of George P. Grant—from the Cave to the Cross and back again with Simone Weil."*

Some overlap occurs where I have included surrounding context from my thesis or expanded essays from *Minerva's Snowy Owl* in their longer forms here. Once again, I have included my complete listing of abbrebiations and bibliography of works consulted for my thesis, though I do not cite many of them in this collection.

# Part 1

# Simone Weil: Red Virgin

# 1

# Simone Weil: George Grant's Diotima

In *We Are Not Our Own*, I contend that Grant's doctrines (contemplative and prophetic) grew from his conversion experience and from his subsequent reflections upon it. This claim is supported by and reflected in his attraction to Weil's work, partly because Weil's work can likewise be regarded as having developed out her own wartime suffering and a religious conversion. Indeed, to understand Grant's sustained spiritual center, Weil's great trials, afflictions, and radical conversion are indispensable.

> His witness during World War II of unlimited innocent suffering (the problem of theodicy) and the atrocities exposed after the War made a lasting impression on him, an impression which found expression in the thought of Weil and her powerful understanding of the afflicted Christ… Grant regarded Weil a saint because she thought the inevitability of Providence and the inevitability of human suffering together and profoundly.[1]

Grant's sustained meditation of Weil's works involved such an internalization of her thoughts that when expressing his own doctrines, he would often lean heavily on her language. These echoes of Weil should not be mistaken for dependence in terms of discovery, since Grant had already apprehended his core truths. However, the correlation of their shared ideas is very strong, more so because the highlights of her conversion journey stirred Grant in ways that would recall his own enlightenment.

### Grant on Weil's conversion accounts

In his 1970 lecture on Weil, he finds it necessary "to say something of those events between 1936 and 1943 whereby God's perfection became immediate to her. (I use the word 'immediate' in the sense that we see each other right now)."[2]

### 1937–38 Assisi / Solesmes

Grant quotes her at length verbatim from her account of awakening in *Waiting for God*.[3] I reproduce it here because of its impact on Grant and by way of comparison to his epiphany and subsequent doctrine.

> In 1937 I had two marvelous days at Assisi. There, alone in this little twelfth-century Romanesque chapel of Santa Maria degli Angeli, an incomparable marvel of purity where Saint Francis often used to pray, *something stronger than I was compelled me for the first in my life to go down on my knees.*
>
> In 1938 I spent ten days at Solesmes, from Palm Sunday to Easter Tuesday, following all the liturgical services. I was suffering from splitting headaches; each sound hurt me like a blow; by an *extreme effort of concentration* I was able to rise above this wretched flesh, to leave it to suffer by itself, heaped up in a corner, and to find a pure and perfect joy in the unimaginable beauty of the chanting and the words. This experience enabled me by analogy to get a better understanding of the possibility of *loving divine love in the midst of affliction.* It goes without saying that in the course of these services the thought of the Passion of *Christ entered into my being once and for all.*
>
> There was a young English Catholic there from whom I gained my first idea of the supernatural power of the sacraments because of the truly angelic radiance with

which he seemed to be clothed after going to communion. Chance—for I always prefer saying chance rather than Providence—made of him a messenger to me. For he told me of the existence of those English poets of the seventeenth century who are named metaphysical. ... It is called "Love".[4] I learned it by heart. Often, at the culminating point of a violent headache, I make myself say it over, *concentrating all my attention*[5] upon it and clinging with all my soul to the tenderness it enshrines. I used to think I was merely reciting it as a beautiful poem, but without my knowing it the recitation had the virtue of a prayer. It was during one of these recitations that, as I told you, *Christ himself came down and took possession of me.*

My arguments about the insolubility of the problem of God had never foreseen the possibility of that, *of a real contact, person to person, here below, between a human being and God.*[6] I had vaguely heard tell of things of this kind, but I had never believed in them. In the Fioretti the accounts of apparitions rather put me off if anything, like the miracles in the Gospel. Moreover, in this *sudden possession of me by Christ*, neither my senses nor my imagination had any part; I only felt in the midst of my suffering the presence of a love, like that which one can read in the smile on a beloved face.[7]

Weil's clear-headed incredulity to actively seeking mystical experiences or flights of imagination that might smell of autosuggestion gave her reports credibility to Grant.[8] He simply believed her. Grant writes,

I, of course, believe that what happened is exactly what she says happened. And this seems to me highly surprising; for I do not like or trust the writings of most mystics and am full of suspicion of their claims. ... Yet I am sure it happened for the reason that what she knows and writes about elsewhere is, I am sure, true, and whatever her faults I cannot think they were those of self-delusion. ... I think that official, institutional Christianity has been quite right in being so firmly suspicious of those claims to direct contact which we call mysticism, because of the obvious and manifold abuses to which they may lead. But when it happens, I am sure it happens, and I am convinced it happened here.[9]

## 1942 Marseilles

One other testimony of Weil's intense spiritual reality, whether literal or literary, bears repeating. It comes from the spring of 1942 in Marseilles. Some ask how this fable should be deciphered.[10] We might better ask, Was Weil prone to fables? Did she not claim a track record of immediate encounters? Does her lifework demonstrate a deluded mind? What if this account were true? And what would we mean by 'true'?

>He entered my room and said: 'Poor creature, you who understand nothing. Come with me and I will teach you things which you do not suspect.' I followed him.

>He took me into a church. It was new and ugly. He led me up to the altar and said: 'Kneel down'. I said 'I have not been baptized'. He said 'Fall on your knees before this place, in love, as before the place where lies the truth'. I obeyed.

>He brought me out and made me climb up to a garret. Through the open window one could see the whole city spread out, some wooden scaffoldings, and the river on which boats were being unloaded. The garret was empty, except for a table and two chairs. He bade me be seated.

>We were alone. He spoke. From time to time someone would enter, mingle in the conversation, then leave again.

>Winter had gone; spring had not yet come. The ranches

of the trees lay bare, without buds, in the cold air full of sunshine.

The light of day would arise, shine forth in splendour, and fade away; then the moon and the stars would enter through the window. And then once more the dawn would come up.

At times he would fall silent, take some bread from the cupboard, and we would share it. This bread really had the tasted of bread. I have never found that taste again.

He would pour out some wine for me, and some for himself—wine which tasted of the sun and of the soil upon which this city was built.

At other times we would stretch ourselves out on the floor of the garret, and sweet sleep would enfold me. Then I would wake and drink in the light of the sun.

He had promised to teach me, but he did not teach me anything. We talked about all kinds of things, in a desultory way, as do old friends.

One day he said to me: 'Now go'. I fell down before him, I clasped his knees, I implored him not to drive me away. But he threw me out on the stairs. I went down unconscious of anything, my heart as if it were in shreds. I wandered along the streets. Then I realized that I had no idea where this house lay.

I have never tried to find it again. I understood that he had come for me by mistake. My place is not in that garret. It can be anywhere—in a prison cell, in one of those middle-class drawing-rooms full of knick-knacks and red plush, in the waiting-room of a station—anywhere except in that garret.

Sometimes I cannot help trying, fearfully and remorsefully, to repeat to myself a part of what he said to me.

> How am I to know if I remember rightly? He is not there to tell me.
>
> I know well that he does not love me. How could he love me? And yet deep down within me something, a particle of myself, cannot help thinking, with fear and trembling, that perhaps, in spite of it all, he loves me.[11]

For Grant's part, he takes this as no fable. When Grant visited Simone's mother in France, Mme. Weil gave him a copy of this testimony. He recounts the experience:

> I have before me Mme Weil's account, in her own handwriting, of when and where he daughter wrote the 'Prologue,' in which she describes how Christ came to her. Mme Weil wrote it out for me, because there had been some historical confusion as to *when the event had occurred.* ... It is a document of lucidity and joy. Any confusion she may have experienced by having brought into the world this eagle was utterly subordinated to her acceptance that her daughter had been *visited in the flesh directly* by Christ.[12]

This was Grant's saint—his prophet—a woman whose experiences and teachings rang true to his understanding and whose major doctrines confirmed what he had come to see and believe.

## Comparison of Grant and Weil's experience

While I compare Grant's conversion to Weil's because of their strikingly similar doctrinal conclusions, Grant himself did not understand his experience to be of the same order. In a 1970 graduate lecture entitled "The Beautiful Itself," Grant contrasted his own life with that of Weil or George Herbert. He flatly denies ever having had a 'mystical experience'—defined as "the immediate [neither through a mediator, nor by inference] appearance of the eternal to human beings."[13] He continues,

> [W]hy I am so unwilling to speak of this [is] because it has not occurred for me. I am not saying that intimations of what such an occurrence would be have not appeared, but the actual occurrence has not... Now the immediacy of this occurrence—mysticism—and the possibility of it being phony or manipulated is why official Western Christianity has been so hesitant and suspicious... [but] The best example of this can be seen in Simone Weil or in George Herbert's poem—'Christ came down and possessed my soul.'[14]

Grant was awestruck by Weil's spiritual experience, the range of her genius, and her radical self-giving. He regarded her as truly God-possessed. He believed her knowledge of God to be direct (mystical), contingent on and confirmed by her life of charity (saintly). He could not claim either for himself.

> I simply want to assert that she claimed to have direct knowledge of the deity and that this direct knowledge is 'in some sense' (at this point undefined) related to her charity. How is one then to give or refuse intellectual assent to doctrines stated by a being who lives in a different level of moral existence from oneself.[15]

> [I]n speaking of her it would be absurd of me to deny that for me in her presence I am not only in the presence of a great thinker but also of sanctity... At the simplest level it is the distance set between herself and myself as commentator who does not live such a life, who has not been called to that terrible destiny, sanctity... That is, the distance between what love has possessed her and my own life.[16]

> For ten years I have been in the horrible position of thinking this position to be true and yet turning away from it. Why do I make this rather egocentric remark? Because the following is true: [quoting Weil] "Human

nature is so constituted that any desire of the soul in so far as it has not passed through the flesh by means of actions and attitudes which correspond to it, has no reality in the soul. It is only there as phantom."[17] ... That is, this doctrine, which I think to be true, I do not consent to it, because I do not consent to it passing through my flesh.[18]

Self-reflection made it clear to Grant that he was neither a saint nor a genius,[19] nor a mystic in the sense that he claimed for Weil. While neither Grant nor others regarded him as a 'holy man,'[20] one might ask:

- Was Grant's self-giving sacrifice in Bermondsey in any way secondary beside Weil's foolhardy taste of the Spanish Civil war, her self-inflicted year in the factory, or her flight from the Nazis into Marseilles? Was he any less courageous?
- Are we to regard Grant's long life of faithful marriage to Sheila at all subordinate to Weil's years of apparent (contested[21]) sexual repression?
- Are Grant's forty-plus years of commitment to the teaching vocation and the advancement of education in Canada diminished by Weil's brief career and contribution in the French classrooms? By what standard? Mere genius?
- Were Grant's political-philosophical insights dim compared to Weil's, especially when we consider the impact of *Lament* on the national scene?
- Was Grant's spiritual awakening actually less direct or life changing than Weil's conversion? How so? Is his involvement as a churchman considered too blasé next to Weil's self-absorbed reticence to join the Church except on her own terms?
- Does Grant's willingness to live as a die-hard proponent and defender of life for seventy years disqualify him from the kind of sainthood conferred on a shooting star like Weil, simply because it lacked

the drama of her early death, arguably a self-righteous suicide by default?
- Are Weil's oft-arcane *Notebooks* superior to Grant's clarity in getting to the heart of the matter? Does posthumous publication elevate their worth?

These questions function, not to diminish Weil's greatness, but to humanize her alongside Grant: remarkably different *and* remarkably similar counterparts in inspired twentieth-century Christian Platonic contemplation and action.

In his devotion to Weil, Grant commenced with an effort to write a synopsis of her thought. His research took him to France in June 1963 for meetings with Weil's mother, Selma, and friend and biographer, Simone Pétrement.[22] He completed all the biographical and literary work for the book[23] but condensed it to an essay for a speech, "Introduction to Simone Weil" (1970) that was not published until 1998 as part of *The George Grant Reader*. Grant cited various reasons for laying aside the project, including specific questions about Weil's thought, Canadian political demands,[24] and the publication of two works that he very much endorsed: M. Veto's *La metaphysique religieuse de Simone Weil* (1971)[25] and Simone Pétrement's, *La vie de Simone Weil.* (1973).[26] But in the end, Grant admits,

> I have not written about SW because at my best I hope what she says is true, but I am also scared that it is true because I am simply not up to it. To be personal, I am lazy, lecherous, self-centred person who knows hardly anything about giving oneself away. It would be presumptuous of me to write of matters of which I know only indirectly.[27]

Ironically, even from Grant's self-disparaging confessions of laziness to his reputation for public pessimism, we hear familiar echoes of Weil.[28]

## Comparison of Grant and Weil's theology

Grant's hagiography of Weil aside, we have two Christian converts whose experiences and reflections lead them to a profundity of similar convictions. They were convinced that modernity had failed miserably. They saw that project come to a dead end in the bloodbath of two world wars and industrial-technological tyranny. They also came independently to parallel doctrines in their contemplative Christian Platonism, their theodicy of the Cross, their prophetic call to social justice, and applied peacemaking in their own contexts. I conclude this essay with a comparison of their key doctrines.

| Weil's Doctrine | Grant's Doctrine |
|---|---|
| i. *Weil names the darkness:*<br>a. Disillusionment with French liberalism.<br>b. The tyranny of factory technology over the workers.<br>c. Disillusionment with her early Marxism. "Revolution … is the Opium of the people."[29] | i. *Naming the darkness as darkness—Grant's deconstruction:*<br>The matrix of modernity. |
| ii. *Faith is the experience of the intellect illumined by love:*<br>a. Weil's 'attention': her embrace of Christian-Platonism.<br>"The wisdom of Plato is not a philosophy, a search for God through human reason. … It is nothing short of a turning of the soul towards grace."[30]<br>"Universal love belongs only to the contemplative faculty of the soul."[31]<br>b. Weil's encounters with Chris*t*. | ii. *The intellect illumined by love—Grant's epistemology:*<br>A contemplative understanding of *noetic* knowledge and the *vita contempletiva*. |

*iii. Torn between the perfection of God and the affliction of man:*

  a. Weil's *malheur* (affliction).
  b. The distance between the Good and necessity, convening only on the Cross.[32]
  c. "It is what it is."

*iv. Love as self-giving consent:*

  a. Not Gnostic (in the flightest sense). "The wise have to return to the cave, and act there."[33]
  b. Engagement in the labour movement, Syndicalism, teaching the poor, Spanish Civil War, factory work, and the French Resistance.

*iii. The perfection of God and the affliction of man—Grant's theology:*

  a. Plato's distance between necessity and the Good
  b. Theodicy of the Cross
  c. Cosmology of Consent

*iv. The love of justice as light in the darkness—Grant's ethics:*

His politics of justice and consent, rooted in an obligation of love for the Good and the other.

## Endnotes

1. Wayne Whillier, "Introduction," *Two Theological Languages* (1990), v.

2. Grant, "Introduction to Simone Weil," *CW* 4: 789.

3. Weil, *WG*, 26v7.

4. LOVE (III) by George Herbert

   Love bade me welcome, yet my soul drew back,
     Guilty of dust and sin.
   But quick-ey'd Love, observing me grow slack
     From my first entrance in,
   Drew nearer to me, sweetly questioning
     If I lack'd anything.
   "A guest," I answer'd, "worthy to be here";
     Love said, "You shall be he."
   "I, the unkind, the ungrateful? ah my dear,
     I cannot look on thee."
   Love took my hand and smiling did reply,
     "Who made the eyes but I?"

> "Truth, Lord, but I have marr'd them; let my shame
>   Go where it doth deserve."
> "And know you not," says Love, "who bore the blame?"
>   "My dear, then I will serve."
> "You must sit down," says Love, "and taste my meat."
>   So I did sit and eat.

5. "Attention consists of suspending our thought, leaving it detached, empty, and ready to be penetrated … our thought should be empty, waiting, not seeking anything, but ready to receive in its naked truth the object that is to penetrate it." (Weil, *WG*, 62).

6. "Sometimes, … Christ is present with me in person, but his presence is infinitely more real, more moving, more clear than on that first occasion when he took possession of me." (Weil, *WG*, 29).

7. Grant, "Introduction to Simone Weil," *CW* 4: 789–90 (citing Weil, *WG*, 26–7).

8. She says, "The imagination is continually at work filling up all the fissures through which grace might pass. … The imagination … is essentially a liar." (Weil, *G&G*, 16).

9. Grant, "Introduction to Simone Weil," *CW* 4: 792.

10. "[T]o my knowledge, no critic has fully elucidated the meaning of the following fable, which she wrote in Marseilles shortly before leaving for the United States." (Francine du Plessix Gray, *Simone Weil* (2001), 229).

11. Weil, *NB* 2: 638–9.

12. Grant, "Review Essay on *Simone Weil: A Modern Pilgrimage*," *CW* 4: 861.

13. Grant, "The Beautiful Itself," *Athens and Jerusalem* (2006), 296.

14. Grant, "The Beautiful Itself," *Athens and Jerusalem* (2006), 296.

15. Grant, "Reading of Simone Weil: Unpublished Excerpt," *MSO*, 199–200.

16. Grant, "Graduate Seminar Lectures on Simone Weil, 1975–6," *CW* 4: 815.

17. Weil, "A Theory of the Sacraments," *G-G*, 65.

18. Grant, "Nietzsche: Graduate Lecture, 1969," *CW* 3: 672–3.

19. He was also a fascinating character, with many vices as he would say. Once he asked me if I had read the Brothers Karamazov and then which character I identified most with. I said rather naively that I was drawn very much to Alyosha. He let out a great guffaw and said, "Oh, I am Dmitri, without a doubt!" (Spencer Estabrooks to Ron Dart, personal correspondence, 07/06/2010).

20. Arati Barua, "George Grant and Gandhi: A Live Interview with Mrs. Sheila Grant," *Grant and Gandhi* (2010), 205.

21. In his review of Robert Coles' *Simone Weil: A Modern Pilgrimage* (1987), Grant says, "Coles writes: 'She had no sexual life.' Simone Weil's closest friend told me in the Gare du Nord in Paris: 'I can tell you that Simone Weil knew human love in its most complete form.'" (Grant, "In Defense of Simone Weil," *CW* 4: 855).

22. GPG to André Weil, 04/22/1963; GPG to Sheila Grant, 06/13/1963; GPG to Sheila Grant, 06/16, 1963 (Christian, *SL*, 216–8).

23. GPG to Principal Salmon, 09/20/1966 (Jersak, *MSO* 14.14).

24. GPG to Sir Richard Rees, 03/31/1967 (Jersak, *MSO* 14.15). Grant was also forced to set aside efforts to translate Weil's *La Connaissance surnaturelle* at this time.

25. GPG to Larry Schmidt, 06/30/1976 (Christian, *SL*, 292).

26. GPG to Simone Pétrement, 04/03/1975 (Christian, *SL*, 282–4).

27. GPG to Joan O'Donovan, 1982 (Christian, *SL*, 323–5).

28. Simone Pétrement, *Simone Weil: A Life* (1976), 176–7, 199, 447.

29. Weil, *G&G*, 181.

30. Weil, *IC*, 85.

31. Weil, *IC*, 194.

32. Grant, *TJ*, 44.

33. Weil, *LP*, 221.

# 2

# Stages of Weil's Mystical Ascent

**Grant's Weil: 'Attention'**

George Grant summarized and defined Simone Weil's contemplative way with her word for it: 'attention' (contra willpower)—a mystical participation in God's love effected by the attentive 'seeing' of love. He says,

> [It] is clear that what [Weil] means by *attention* is certainly the means whereby human beings move to participate in supernatural love; it also has to do with the question concerning sight in the metaphor of the Sun, and the question of whether sight is to be taken as love or intelligence.[1]

As one gathers the strands of Weil's contemplative process from her journals, articles and books, a 'Weilian contemplative path' emerges. Once discovered, it compares with and rivals the grand mystical paths of history, including ancients (Plato, the Buddha, Christ), pre-moderns (Teresa of Avila, John of the Cross, Meister Eckhart), and contemporaries (Evelyn Underwood, Thomas Merton). I suggest that Weil's 'attention' unfolds in five stages: (i) ascent, (ii) arrest, (iii) attention, (iv) awakening, and (v) activation. This model emphasizes the epistemological impasse where the rational mind finds its limits and the love-illumined *nous* waits for the grace-gift of enlightenment.

For an impression of its grandeur, we must see the whole in outline before I offer my comments. For the sake of brevity, I will also label without comment Weil's conscious parallels between Plato's cave and St. John of the Cross.[2]

| Mystical Stage | Contemplative Practice | Objects of Attention |
|---|---|---|
| **i. Ascent:** Climb from the cave. | a. Ascent by **attention** to the limits of reason | Attention to affliction<br>Attention to beauty<br>Attention to math irrationals |
| (John of the Cross: Dark Night of the Soul – *FLN* 242) | b. Ascent by **attention** to contradictories | Apparent contradictions<br>Incommensurates<br>Mysteries |
| | c. Ascent by **acceptance** (i.e., decreation of the ego) | Obedience to necessity (*amor fati*)<br>Consent to affliction<br>Allowing the void |
| | d. Ascent by **love** (of God) | Religious ritual<br>Beauty (God's trap)<br>Love of neighbour<br>Friendship |

| | | |
|---|---|---|
| **ii. Arrest:** Halted at the threshold.<br><br>(John of the Cross: Dark Night of the Spirit – *FLN* 243) | a. **Attention creates an *impasse*:** love, beauty and affliction arrests us with astonishment (blinded by the light)<br><br>b. **Acceptance preserves a *void*:** consent creates a space for the divine and human other (otherness = presence)<br><br>c. **Implicit love** prepares us for *direct contact* | The mystic ascends to the top of the noetic ladder, where she can only stop, watch, and wait for grace |
| **iii. Attention:** Waiting for the light. | Second Ascent by **attention** (faculty of love) | Waiting for God<br><br>Desiring, not willing<br><br>Asking, seeking, knocking |
| **iv. Awakening:** Beholding the Sun.<br><br>(John of the Cross: Mystical Union) | a. **Contact**<br>b. **Mediation** (*metaxu*)<br>c. **Possession** | The same love that drew one up the ladder, brings God down to lift one up |
| **v. Activation:** Return to the cave. | a. **True vision** never leaves the world<br>b. **True attention** on the world is participation in God<br>c. **True knowledge** is charity | Knowledge, even of God, is not reality until it 'passes through the flesh' by actions of charity |

### i. Ascent: Climb from the cave

Ascent—from chains to threshold—occurs for the contemplative who desires to leave the cave (belief in the temporal alone), and, by employing the faculty of intelligence (the *nous*) at this stage, embarks on a means of deliberate progress through a course of attention, acceptance, and love.

Grant explains how Weil's model of attention leads to decreation, a Christ-like emptying of selfish purposes and denunciation of mastery (i.e., Jesus' 'poverty of spirit').

> In turning out from ourselves towards the exterior it empties our spirit of the purposes of self. We are all taken up in our own experiences. Attention empties us of these purposes and therefore leads to decreation. ... In thinking of this I was reminded of St Paul's great phrase in Philippians 2:11, 'Christ who being in the form of God, counted it not prize to be equal with God but emptied himself ...' That is what attention is from its simplest to its highest, the emptying of self of its purposes, its sense of autonomy.[3]

Weil begins with giving our full attention to the limits of reason and to simultaneous contraries. Later, we'll see that attention elevated by love to gaze upon the Sun (God, the Good, universals).

a. *Ascent by attention to the limits of reason.* At this first stage, like *gelassenheit*, attention is open and attentive, but refrains from willful expectations that could box in the truth or impose ourselves upon it:

> Attention consists of suspending our thought, leaving it *detached, empty and ready to be penetrated* by the object. It means holding in our minds, within reach of this thought, but on a lower level and not in contact with it, the diverse knowledge we have acquired which we are

forced to make use of. Above all our thought should be *empty, waiting, not seeking anything*, but *ready to receive* in its naked truth the object which is to penetrate it. All wrong translations, all absurdities in geometry problems, all clumsiness of style and all faulty connection of ideas ... all such things are due to the fact that thought has seized upon some idea too hastily and being thus prematurely blocked, is not open to truth. The cause is always that we have wanted to be too active; we have wanted to carry out a search."[4]

In Weil's attention, the *nous* (intelligence) is exercised to explore the outer *limits of reason*, hoping by experience to ascend the noetic ladder to its topmost rung. "Reason should exercise its function of demonstration only in order to succeed in stumbling up against the true mysteries, the true indemonstrables, which are the real."[5]

Weil identifies particular objects of attention where the human mind can come to this state of arrest: attention to affliction,[6] attention to beauty,[7] and attention to certain types of math/physics (e.g., irrational numbers[8]). All of these, if one has the stamina for extreme attention, can draw the contemplative to states of mind-numbing speechlessness where *dianoia* is overwhelmed and we are halted into the higher waiting attention of love.

b. *Ascent by attention to contradiction*. Weil is especially voluminous on the power of attention on *contradiction* or 'simultaneous contraries' to arrest us. Contradiction functions like the Buddhist *koan*[9] to create double-binds that act as pincers to draw the soul beyond its rational capacities towards the light of the Good.[10] Weil says, "The contemplation of these absurdities draws one upwards, if they are contemplated as *absurd* (they must not then be defended)."[11]

Eric Springsted has identified three layers of contradiction for attention within Weil's work.[12] First, *apparent contradictions* that can be resolved by analysis and proper predication of the opposing terms involved. Second, *incommensuration*, defined as the comparison of two things that have no common intellectual measure. The terms cannot be so resolved, but a unity of the set is discoverable at a higher plane than the one in which the elements are incommensurate.[13] She calls this the Pythagorean harmony of contraries.[14] And third, *mystery*, where we ponder incommensurates that seem inextricably linked, yet without our being able to comprehend that in which their unity lies.[15] The examples that appear repeatedly in Weil's work focus on issues of theodicy, examined in detail in the next chapter. For now, consider these examples from her work:

- "I have been ceaselessly torn by the perfection of God and the affliction of man and the relation between the two."[16]
- "God is the cause of everything. God is only the cause of good."[17]
- "Cases of true contradictories: God exists; God doesn't exist."[18]

By attention—not rational solution and not suppression—such mysteries offer their gift: potential passage beyond the threshold, out from the cave.

> The notion of mystery is legitimate when the most logical and rigorous use of the intelligence leads to an impasse, to a contradiction which is inescapable in this sense: that the suppression of one term makes the other meaningless and that to pose one term necessarily involves posing the other. Then, like a lever, the notion of mystery carries thought beyond the impasse, to the other side of the un-openable door, beyond the domain of intelligence and above it. But to arrive beyond the domain of the intelligence one must have travelled all through it, to the end, and by a path traced with unimpeachable rigor ... by a long and loving contemplation.[19]

c. *Ascent by acceptance*. Besides the practice of attention, Weil also believed in the contemplative power of practicing acceptance.

> The duty of acceptance in all that concerns the will of God, whatever it may be, was impressed upon my mind as the first and most necessary of all duties from the time when I found it set down in Marcus Aurelius under the form of the *amor fati* of the Stoics.[20]

To her this meant loving the universe "in the total integrity of the order and necessity which are its substance, and all the events that occur in it."[21] It includes complete and unconditional consent to the absolute Good,[22] to God's work of re-creating us and de-creating us,[23] and consent even where God leaves us to the mechanical operations of this world ('impersonal providence'), not as blind force but as submission to the universal Wisdom of God's good order.[24] Weil insists that this consent extends even to extreme affliction, which alone brings complete redemptive suffering.[25]

A caveat: when we or our loved ones or neighbours undergo affliction, she says, it must be in spite of ourselves, having done whatever we can to prevent the pain and even begging God for another way (as Christ did), for 'death is what is required, not suicide.'[26] Weil is explicit: it is wrong to desire it, against nature, a perversion, because by nature, affliction is suffered unwillingly.[27] But when affliction inevitably descends, we practice *amor fati* (literally, 'love of fate') or what Weil called the supreme virtue of 'obedience to necessity.' If we allow suffering do its decreating work in us, a *void* is opened for God's Spirit.[28] We attain 'nakedness of spirit' that God's love will fill without fail.[29] Becoming nothing, we become everything.[30] Acceptance in affliction thus acts as a reliable lever so that the lower we go, the higher we ascend, without any effort except detaching from our desire to will our way up.[31] If we persevere in love, even when the soul cries, "My God, why have you forsaken me," Weil promises that we will "end by touching something that is not our affliction … the very love of God."[32]

Weil gathers all of these themes in a few lines reproduced in *Gravity and Grace*:

> The extinction of desire (Buddhism)—or detachment—or *amor fati*—or desire for the absolute good—these all amount to the same: to empty desire, finality of all content, to desire in the void, to desire without any wishes.
>
> To detach our desire from all good things and to wait. Experience proves that this waiting is satisfied. It is then we touch the absolute good.[33]

I pause to critique Weil's use of *amor fati*, not because I find fault with it in theory or in practice.[34] Indeed, Weil's depiction of Christianity and Stoicism as sharing some ideas (humility, obedience, and love) and language (*logos*, *pneuma*) may be quite correct.[35] But while the ancient Stoics or modern recovery movements promise that practicing acceptance will lead to peace and serenity, one of Weil's letters describes a disturbing side-effect in her own life.

> The result was that the irreducible quantity of hatred and repulsion which goes with suffering and affliction recoiled entirely upon myself. And the quantity is very great, because the suffering in question is located at the very root of my every single thought without exception.
>
> This is so much the case that I absolutely cannot imagine the possibility that any human being could feel friendship for me.[36]

How do we process this testimony? It sounds as though she either came into an experience of fellowship with the redemptive sufferings of Christ such that she too became a curse (Gal. 3:13), *or* decreation had not yet marginalized her ego-voices of self-hatred and repulsion. On this, Weil herself must function for us as a *koan*.

d. *Ascent by love*. At this stage of ascent, along with attention and acceptance, the contemplative is also called to participate in what Weil calls the 'implicit love of God.' Weil responds to the commandment, "Thou shalt love the Lord thy God," (Deut. 6:5 KJV) by describing the call to indirect love of [for] God that precedes direct contact with God 'in person.' She explains: "This previous love cannot have God for its object, since God is not present to the soul and has never yet been so. It must then have another object. Yet it is destined to become the love of God."[37] In her essay, "Forms of the Implicit Love of God," she enumerates four of these 'veiled loves' that serve as preparatory for the explicit revelation (direct contact) of the Divine Bridegroom's nuptial love. These forms of attentive love include love of neighbour, love of the beauty and order of the world, love of religious practices, and friendship. Each implicit love acts in the manner of a sacrament, bearing and mediating the presence of Christ between lover and beloved.

Weil's *love of neighbour* draws from Jesus in Matthew 25, where he says, "I was hungry and you fed me. ... What you did for the least of these my brothers and sisters, you did for me." To Weil, the presence of God is Christ in the sufferer, in the benefactor, and in the bread given in compassion, so that God himself loves God through this entire act of real communion.[38] God descends to the afflicted, present as supernatural, personal love in those animated by genuine charity (in the ancient sense). Love of neighbour is love of God, fulfilling the two great commandments simultaneously and defining true justice.[39]

*Love of the beauty* or order of the world, according to Weil, is the most natural, easiest approach to the implicit love of God. "The soul's natural inclination to love beauty is the trap God most frequently uses in order to win it and open it to the breath from on high."[40] She describes it as a labyrinth into which we are drawn ever more deeply, where God is waiting to devour us! We come out again, but are changed and thereafter, linger at the mouth of the labyrinth in order to nudge others inside.

Says Weil,

> God created the universe, and his Son, our first-born brother, created the beauty in it for us. The beauty of the world is Christ's tender smile for us coming through matter. He is really present in the universal beauty. The love of this beauty proceeds from God dwelling in our souls and goes out to God present in the universe. It is also a sacrament.[41]

*Love of religious practices* is another form of indirect love for God, since it too is a mediated love. The foundation of religious practice at its best, according to Weil, is an invitation to transformation by pronouncing the name of God (e.g., Buddhism), and/or purification by looking on perfect purity (e.g., the Eucharist). The means of appropriation is 'attention animated by desire' whereby we make contact with God's love. Thus, "the part of evil in the soul is burned by the fire of this contact and becomes only suffering, and the suffering is impregnated with love."[42]

Weil is anxious that we should understand that even religious practice is not a matter of religious will-power—neither moral rigor nor ritualistic gymnastics—but of waiting desire. Her model is the bronze serpent in the Hebrew wilderness narrative (as it was for Jesus in the third chapter of John's Gospel):

> One of the principal truths of Christianity, a truth that goes almost unrecognized today, is that looking is what saves us. The bronze serpent was lifted up so that those who lay maimed in the depths of degradation should be saved by looking upon it. ... The effort that brings a soul to salvation is like the effort of looking or of listening; it is the kind of effort by which a fiancée accepts her

lover. It is an act of attention and consent; whereas what language designates as will is something suggestive of muscular effort. ... The weeds are pulled up by the muscular effort of the peasant, but only sun and water can make the corn grow. The will cannot produce any good in the soul"[43]

Thus, 'passive activity' or 'non-acting action' (cf. the Bhagavad-Gita and Lao-Tse) should be the posture of the religious supplicant.[44]

*Friendship*. Almost as an afterthought, Weil reflects on the love of God experienced in friendship. It is "a personal and human love which is pure and which enshrines an intimation and a reflection of divine love."[45] Friendship differs from charity in that it involves preference, and so always risks self-seeking attachments of neediness, restraint, or domination that would keep us from the greater good of the 'free disposal' of ourselves.[46] But pure friendship is an occasion for 'equality made of harmony' (rather than sameness), for the 'supernatural miracle of respect for human autonomy,' and therefore also, a sacramental 'image of the original and perfect friendship' of the Trinity.[47]

These implicit forms of love for God—love of neighbour, beauty, ritual, and friend—draw the soul upward to the threshold of direct contact with God, which once accomplished, does not disband these previous loves, but makes them wholly real.

### ii. Arrest: Halted at the threshold

Through attention, acceptance, and the implicit love of God, the Weilian mystic climbs to the terminal rung of the noetic ladder, to the very limits of Kantian 'knowledge' and modernity's boundaries of 'reality.' The Platonic prisoner comes to the doorway of the cave, where the soul is arrested. 'Climbing' further is impossible. The contemplative can now only stop, watch and wait for grace. To review the education of the soul to this point:

a. *Attention to love, beauty and affliction has arrested the pilgrim soul with astonishment.*[48] Blinded by the first glimpses of sunlight, fleeing or flailing avails us nothing. We must simply wait for our spiritual eyes to adjust to a direct vision of reality.

b. *Acceptance and surrender have weakened the ego, creating and preserving a void within.* As with God at creation and Christ's incarnation and passion, persistent love through consent has carved a space for the divine presence and the human other. Paradoxically, mysteriously, the absence of God welcomes and mediates the immanent presence of God.

c. *Implicit love has prepared the soul for a greater level of attention with a newfound capacity for direct contact.* The attention of the intelligence defers to the attention of the higher faculty of love, which turns to welcome the overtures of divine love and been drawn up into it the light of God.

In the imagery of Plato's cave, we have come to the threshold. Weil extends the metaphor to include all the above themes in a profound little poem, in startling parallel to George Grant's 'gateway conversion.' Without a doubt, its poignancy would have gripped him.

### The Threshold[49]

Open the door to us, and we will see the orchards,
We will drink their cold water where the moon
    has left its trace.
The long road burns, hostile to strangers.

We wander without knowing and find no place.
We want to see flowers. Here thirst grips us.
Waiting and suffering, we are here before the door.
If we must, we will break this door with our fists.
We press and push, but the barrier still holds.

One must weaken, must wait and look vainly.
We look at the door: it is closed, unbreachable.

We fix our eyes there; we weep under the torment;
We see it always; the weight of time crushes us.

Before us is the door; what use for us to wish?
Better to turn away, abandoning hope.
We will never enter. We are weary of seeing it …
The door, opening, let so much silence escape.

That neither the orchards appeared nor any flower;
Only the immense space where emptiness and
    light are
Was suddenly everywhere present, overflowed
    the heart,
And washed our eyes almost blind under the dust.

And so we gaze at the threshold of the cave—where Grace now causes us to emerge.[50]

### iii. Attention (to the eternal): Waiting for the light

As Grant understood her, Weil's epistemological pilgrimage works this way: the attention of the intelligence is activated when grace breaks the chains of delusion and we first see the light of the fire in Plato's cave. We make our ascent through the realm of necessity (the cave) to the threshold of the realm of the Good, where love alone can behold God. The continuity between the ascent of intelligence and the ascent of love is attention.[51] The discontinuity lies in what each faculty can apprehend:

> Supernatural love, although its function is not to affirm, constitutes a fuller apprehension of reality than does the intelligence, and this is known through the intelligence itself, in the soul in which supernatural love exists; for if it does not exist, the intelligence is unable to pronounce with regard to it.
>
> We know through the intelligence that what the intelligence does not apprehend is more real than what it does apprehend.[52]

In Weil's words, this attention includes waiting (not willing) and looking (i.e., loving) for truth/God to come:

> People who make athletic leaps towards heaven are too absorbed in the muscular effort to be able to look up to heaven; and in this matter the looking up is the one thing that counts. It is what makes God come down. And when God has come down to us he raises us, he gives us wings. ... God alone is the elevating power, and he comes when we look towards him. To look towards him means to love him. There is no other relation between man and God except love. But our love for God should be like a woman's love for a man, which does not express itself by making advances but consists only in waiting.[53]

So attention is very much related to desire (but not effort) for truth and love for God.

> Attention is akin to philosophy, a love of truth. Attention requires desire for truth, which is God. Like all desire, attention cannot be driven by effort, but is motivated by the joy of truth seeking. The burning desire that drives attention purifies the soul.[54]

In her notebooks, Weil exhorts herself to "that attention which is so full that the 'I' disappears ... I have to deprive all that I call 'I' of the light of my attention and turn it on to that which cannot be conceived."[55] This type of attention is synonymous with humility, with supplication. In fact, she says, "Attention, taken to its highest degree, is the same thing as prayer. It presupposes faith and love. ... We should pay attention to such a point that we no longer have the choice."[56]

In the poem above, the waiting soul experiences the despair of a delay after detaching from the world but before it has attached itself to God. Weil describes it as "void, terrible anguish ... solitude without any intermediary," and frequently compares it to St. John of the Cross's 'dark night.'[57] However long it may take,

It is not for man to go towards God, it is for God to go towards man. Man has only to watch and wait. [God] only enters into contact with the individual human being as such by means of purely spiritual grace which responds to the gaze turned toward him, that is to say, to the precise degree in which the individual ceases to be one.[58]

### iv. Awakening: Beholding the Sun

With patient and diligent attention, the soul comes to a *kairos* moment, and *suddenly* experiences a grace-awakening that sparks contact with the divine. Plato says, "as a result of continued application to the subject itself and communion therewith, it is brought to birth in the soul *on a sudden*, as light that is kindled by a leaping spark, and thereafter it nourishes itself."[59] The temporal/finite are raised to behold the eternal; the transcendent is made immanent (through intermediaries or *metaxu*[60]); the eternally wide chasm between the necessary and the Good is bridged.

a. *Contact*. Weil explains how attention leads to contact. "It is the highest part of the attention which makes contact with God. When prayer is intense and pure enough for such a contact to be established, the whole attention is turned towards God."[61] "This seems a contradiction in terms, and yet the transcendent can only be known through contact, since our faculties are unable to construct it."[62] This understanding represents Weil's mystical experience, and also her interpretation of Plato's revelation. We see what the Apostle Peter called 'participation in the divine nature' (2 Pet. 1:4) in Plato's *Phaedrus*. Note this excerpt from Weil's commentary on *Phaedrus*:

> "*The essential property of wings is to lift up what is heavy.*" (*Phaedrus*, 246d). It would be impossible to state more clearly that the wing is a *supernatural organ*, that it is *grace*.

> "*It rises in the air, up to the place where dwells the race of the gods; and of all bodily things it is the one which has most affinity with the divine. The divine is beautiful, wise, good, and so forth; and these are the virtues which particularly nourish and foster the winged part of the soul.* (*Phaedrus*, 246d) ...
>
> "*Just as God's thought is nourished by pure spirit and knowledge* (νοῦς καί ἐπιστήμη) *so also is the thought of every soul which is on the point of receiving its rightful inheritance; when, across time, it perceives reality, it loves* (ἀγαπᾷ) *and contemplates and feeds on truth and is happy.*" (*Phaedrus*, 247d–e)
>
> N.B. It is obvious here what Plato means by the Ideas. They are purely and simply *the attributes of God*.
>
> "*Such is the life of the gods. And among the other souls, the best of them will follow God and resemble him and will lift the charioteer's head up into the world beyond the sky, and the soul ...* " (*Phaedrus*, 248a).[63]

b. *Mediation*: Plato talked about the great difference between the necessary and the Good.[64] Contact across that distance requires mediation. Weil believed that Greek civilization was one grand quest for bridges (*metaxu*) to span the gulf between human misery and God's perfection.[65] Indeed, seeing the centrality of mediation in Plato is one of Weil's great contributions to Plato studies.[66] Emmanuel Gabellieri describes the three pillars of Weil's Platonic Christology as the three *metaxu* of Suffering (*Republic* and *Prometheus*), Beauty (*Symposium*), and the World Order (*Timaeus*)—each 'a modality of love' hidden in Christ as mediator.[67] For Weil, in the end, mediation must be a work of God. Weil says, "God is mediation, and all mediation is God. ... One cannot pass from nothing to nothing without passing through God. God is the unique path. He is the way."[68]

In the next chapter, we will see how the Cross represents ultimate mediation[69]—the intersection of necessity and the Good, of Creator and creation, of time and eternity. This is not merely something we come to 'know' or 'see'—or if we do, such knowledge/sight involves *total* participation.

> He whose soul remains ever turned toward God though the nail pierces it finds himself nailed to the very center of the universe. It is the true center; it is not in the middle; it is beyond space and time; it is God. ... It is at the intersection of creation and its Creator. The point of intersection is the point of intersection on the arms of the Cross.[70]

Though Christ is the fulfillment of this Platonic idea, it *is* nevertheless Platonic—a Platonism beyond dualism in its discovery of Socrates' essential model of mediation (*metaxu*) and participation (*methexis*).[71]

c. *Possession*: For Weil, the contemplative walk leads to an epistemological awakening, to contact with reality, and to participation in the divine nature. Weil, as always, finds a stronger word yet: we are not talking about a search, but rather, a 'possession' whereby we finally come to truly know and be:

> To search is to impede rather than to facilitate God's operation. The man of whom God has *taken possession* no longer searches at all in the sense which Pascal seems to use the word search. ... We must only wait and call out. Not call upon someone, while we still do not know if there *is* anyone; but cry out that we are hungry and want bread. Whether we cry for a long time or a short time, in the end we shall be fed, and then we shall not believe but we shall *know* that there really is bread.[72]

'Possession' is rather dramatic language, but it mirrors Christ's 'Not my will, but thine,' and Grant's 'We are not our own.' It is the word Weil associates with her conversion. It describes the clinging, gazing love of someone whose heart is ravished. And in the case of God, leads us to internalize God's own character. That is, we participate in God's goodness, beauty, truth, and justice—in God's ravished heart for humanity. Thus, true knowledge in Plato's sense is about meeting God, being indwelt by God, and so, becoming like God.

> The followers of Zeus desire that their beloved should have a soul like him ... because they have been compelled to gaze intensely on him; their recollection clings to him, and they become possessed of him, and receive from him their character and disposition, so far as man can *participate in God*.[73]

Grant, in my view, entirely accepted Weil's Platonic epistemology. Especially that true knowledge is the intelligence illumined by love and the soul released from the cave to participate in the divine nature. Whatever knowledge of reality is available can never be grasped by the will, but only received by grace through love of the Good. He, like Weil, saw Socrates as a forerunner of Christ, whose life work was to mediate necessity and the Good by uniting divine perfection and human affliction on a Cross.

### v. Activation: Return to the cave

We return to an earlier Weilian theme: the idea that true knowledge is *not* complete with one's ascent to the divine vision, but by an incarnation of the Good in the world through love. Would it not be glorious if the contemplative could come to an awakening where the soul is released from the fetters of humanity and assimilated into the nirvana of God's light and love! Would not that be the ultimate good?

It is *possible* to read fragments of Plato and even Christ that might give that impression. But from Weil and Grant, as from Christ and Plato, we hear a resounding "No!" For Plato, epistemology is not finally fulfilled in the vision of the Sun, but in the surprising love-compelled return to the cave. Moreover, it is not from the fetters of humanity that we are freed, but from the delusion that temporality is the whole story. Nor is the return to the cave solely for the benefits of the prisoners. The contemplative vision (as epistemology) is crowned by experiencing the depths of beauty and affliction in the world, by seeing the world (through God's eyes), and by being in the world (through charity). In other words, *only by returning to the cave do we fully escape the cave.*

Weil once said, "Human nature is so arranged that a desire of the soul, unless it *passes through the flesh* by means of actions, movements and postures that naturally correspond to it, hasn't any reality for the soul. It dwells there only as a phantom."[74] That is, we don't know reality until we live it in the flesh. Here, Eric Springsted, at the forefront of Weilian scholarship, says,

> For Weil, in the strictest sense we never transcend construction in this world; even the philosopher who leaves the cave returns, and indeed must return as a direct consequence of whatever vision of the Good she has had. ... As Weil notes, the *Timaeus* is the book of one who has returned to the cave; ... Vision and understanding never leave the world. Rather we are always "reading" the world.[75] [I.e., we have a perspective.]

In other words, the Platonic vision (seeing/knowing) is more than a construction. It sees reality, but always from a perspective. This can't be helped. But the contemplative is one who has climbed the ladder of Platonic knowledge from reverie to opinion to reason to intelligence to love, where one's 'reading' is ultimately illumined with wisdom. Thus for Weil, "[W]isdom is an underlying moral stance from which we read the world. It is, for example, to look at the world justly—as it is and not as we would like it to be."[76] I conclude from this (thanks to Springsted):

a. *The true vision—the highest knowing illumined by love—never leaves the world.* It leaves, rather, the delusional view of the world enclosed in a cavern of excluded knowledge/nominalism. Seeing the bigger picture (the whole), encountering the higher forms, and loving God does not negate the reality, value, or beauty of temporal existence. Instead, it floods them with light so that we can see the sacred essence of all things. Weil says, "To love God, to think on God, is nothing else than a certain way of thinking on the world."[77] And, "It is not the way a man talks about God, but the way he talks about the things of this world that best shows whether his soul has passed through the fire of the love of God."[78]

b. *True attention on the world is participation in God.* Springsted is quick to clarify: we are not talking about a purely internal experience where we gaze on metaphysical objects in a private inner world. Nor are we reducing Plato's vision to a subjective perspective of the outer world. Rather, the Christian Platonic tradition testifies to overcoming an inner/outer dualism:

> The one who dwells in the inner is the one who has actually overcome the distinction. Her 'spiritual knowledge' is the way she looks at the world as a whole. This does not mean that the knowledge of God is nothing more than a way of looking at the world; but it does mean that it is linking and inseparable from it. *Looking at the world attentively and wisely, one participates in God.*[79]

c. *True knowledge is charity.* This participation in God via life in the world takes the contemplative to the pinnacle of true knowledge: charity. Weil says,

> It is only in so far as the soul orients itself towards what ought to be loved, ... in so far as it loves God, that it is *qualified to know and understand.* Man cannot exert his intelligence to the full without *charity,* because the only source of light is God. Therefore the faculty of su-

pernatural love is higher than the intelligence and is its condition.[80]

Grant, as he does so frequently, reiterates Weil in this combination of love-illumined intelligence, knowing the Good, and what he likes to call 'love of one's own.'

> If faith is the experience that the intelligence is illuminated by love, then how can human beings learn to love if the beginning of love is not love of one's own? It is in this sense that I think *love of one's own is connected to love of the good*. It is not the element of possession or of extension of the self, which makes one's "own" important, but rather its availability for *being known* by us, and *known as good*.[81]

The pattern for the epistemology of love is Plato's just man and Jesus of the Gospels. They are *made perfect* by incarnating charity and manifesting justice in the hostile context of the proverbial cave, even to the point of suffering humiliation and death. The author of Hebrews, reflecting on Jesus, notes, "Son though he was, he *learned* obedience from what he suffered and, once *made perfect*, he *became the source* of eternal salvation for all who obey him" (Heb. 5:8–9). 'Learning,' being 'made perfect,' and 'becoming' are surprising verbs to describe the same Jesus whom the same author says is "the same yesterday, today, and forever" (Heb. 13:8). The point again undermines every dualism: God / the Good is perfect and cannot be more perfect, but this perfection must be *manifest* in the temporal world or it is *not* perfection. Moreover, that perfection is intimately related to the 'suffering of love,' of which Grant says, "the intelligence's enlightenment by love is a terrible teaching (in the literal sense of the word). Contemplate what happens to those who have been deeply illuminated by love!"[82]

The contemplative who has truly been awakened must be illumined by love, and that love, according to Grant and Weil, is only perfected in action (charity) in the world. By bringing the light of supernatural love into the world, the world truly becomes the real world. After a brief analysis, this will bring us to Grant's Christ.

**vi. Analysis**

Three ponderables present in the wake of Weil's stages:

a. *How well does Weil's epistemology reflect Plato?* It is debatable, for Weilian Platonism aggressively seeks 'intimations of Christianity' in Plato. To a degree this is fair if we see him as a forerunner whose ideas inform Christian doctrine in helpful ways, but she seems almost desperate to read Trinitarian faith back into Greeks who intended no such thing. At most we can concede that Trinitarian Christianity need not abandon Plato completely as incompatible to it, but many Christians have always largely believed that.

Still, I would argue that Weil's research and reflection should at the least make it impossible for another generation of scholars to conceive of Plato as a rationalist or his dialogues as logocentric. Moreover, she has uniquely highlighted the centrality of love to the vision of the Good and its interdependence with knowledge in Plato's thought. Its inexplicable invisibility for thinkers like Heidegger is no longer excusable. That is, the more broadly read Weil becomes, the deeper her permanent impact will be for Plato scholarship. We may disagree with her mystical read of Plato, but we ought not ignore it.

b. *Does Weil's epistemology accurately represent Grant's understanding?* Grant answers for himself: "There is a phrase of Simone Weil's that faith is the experience that the intelligence is enlightened by love. I am trying to think what this means. That's what all my thoughts are turned on now."[83] The later Grant became ever more explicit about his dependence on Weil—especially her Christian Platonism—until she is no longer a silent partner.[84]

> Simone Weil … has been the greatest influence in my life of any thinker. She has shown me what it is to hold Christ and Plato together. She has shown me how sanctity and philosophy can be at one. … I take her writings as combining the staggering clarity of her French education with divine inspiration. I take them as perhaps occasionally mistaken in detail, and as sometimes beyond me, but as the great teaching concerning the eternal in this era.[85]

It is fair to say, to the degree Grant could follow her epistemology, Weil speaks for him. His one fleeting critique of her work on attention is her use of the language of 'object.'

> One point where I think her language is less wise than Heidegger's is her constant use of the word 'object.' She was brought up in the French Cartesian language of subjects-objects; one has already entered the thinking with 'will' in German, and this clearly applies to English because of being forced to give its reasons. We summon it forth.[86]

We see here Grant's awareness of Descartes, Bacon, and Kant, lurking in the assumed language of 'object' that leads to mastery. In Weil's use of hard attention on an 'object' other than oneself in order to decreate oneself, Grant seems to think the language concedes too much to the origins of modern knowing.

Where I would question Weil's contemplative outline would be in the typical experiential shift from description to prescription—from 'this is what happened to me' to 'this is what we should do.' In fact, trying to recapitulate an experience of grace by mimicking the symptoms of grace sends one back into striving (e.g., God touched me, so I shook and wept. You should shake and weep so that God will touch you). In fact, Grant's (and even Weil's) actual experiences were more spontaneous and limited compared to the meticulously staged outline above. Their conversions were sudden and intrusive, certainly the result of decreation and arrest, but wholly undirected and unexpected. Their commitment to 'attention' must not be mistaken for monastic discipline. Their 'attentive openness' is probably more akin to a brooding temperament amidst the chaos of tragedy that led them to both let go and hang on. That is, they relinquished the assumptions of progressivism and abandoned the Enlightenment project. At the same time, for all their openness, Grant and Weil were stubbornly convinced through their contemplations and experiences of Plato and Christ's God of love.

c. *To the degree that Grant's Platonism is expressed in Weil, what does Grant contribute? Or is he merely a derivative thinker?*[87] Hardly. While Grant's analysis of Plato keeps in lockstep with Weil, on one hand he is less wild in his speculations, and on the other, he can break new ground where she could or would not. Two examples:

First, unlike Weil, he was willing to face Nietzsche's genius head-on, pitting Plato's Good and Christ's love against Nietzsche's will to power. She was too repulsed by Nietzsche's supposed arrogance to take seriously his contributions and challenges.[88] Conversely, once Grant discovered Nietzsche, he never wrote another book without referencing his influence, with both kudos and critiques.

Second, while Weil only occasionally references the existentialists and *dasein*,[89] Grant will have decades to engage with the work of Sartre and Heidegger in a serious and expanded way. He contrasts and correlates their philosophical and contemplative insights with that of Weil and Plato, applying them to his own cultural and historical context.

### Endnotes

1. Grant, "Excerpts from Graduate Seminar Lectures," *CW* 4: 826–7.

2. Weil, *NFR*, 264; Weil, *NB* 324, 336, 545.

3. Grant, "Excerpts from Graduate Seminar Lectures," *CW* 4: 829.

4. Weil, *WG*, 111–12.

5. Florence de Lussy, "To On" (2004), 127 (citing Simone Weil, K11, ms. 42).

6. E.g., Weil, *SNL*, 170–98.

7. E.g., Weil, *G&G*, 148–54.

8. E.g., Weil, "Notes on Cleanthes, Pherecydes, Anaximander, and Philolaus," *SNL*, 142, where she takes the irrationals discovered by the Pythagoreans as divine in origin and mediated to us by geometry.

9. Weil, *NB* 2: 396–7, 399, 446, 454, 462, 483, 494.

10. Weil, *NB* 1: 34; 2: 394.

11. Weil, *NB* 1: 243.

12. Eric O. Springsted, "Contradiction, Mystery, and the Use of Words in Simone Weil," *Paying Attention to the Sky* (2010).

13. Weil, *NB* 2: 410.

14. Weil, *IC*, 148.

15. Weil, *FLN*, 109.

16. Grant, "Course Lectures at McMaster," *CW* 3: 727. Grant's paraphrase of a letter from Weil to Maurice Schummann, 1943(?) (Weil, *7OL*, 178).

17. Weil, *NB* 1: 254.

18. Weil, *NB* 1: 127.

19. Weil, *FLN*, 181.

20. Weil, *WG*, 24.

21. Weil to Joe Bousquet, 05/12/1942 (Weil, *7OL*, 142).

22. Weil, *NB* 2: 404–5.

23. Weil, *NB* 2: 545.

24. Weil, *NFR*, 286. A study contrasting Nietzsche and Weil's use of *amor fati*, though fascinating, lays outside the purview of this work.

25. Weil, *NB* 1: 258; Weil, *NFR*, 262–3.

26. Weil, *NB* 1: 258.

27. Weil, *G-G*, 87–8.

28. Cf. Grant on Weil's conception of attention, decreation and the void, *CW* 4: 827–8.

29. Weil, *NB* 1: 96, 150 (obedience to necessity, not to force), 227, 258.

30. Weil, *NB* 1: 120, 123, 130; 2: 467.

31. Weil, *NB* 1: 156, 163, 169.

32. Weil, *WG*, 44.

33. Weil, *G&G*, 13.

34. E.g., as practiced in 12-step recovery literature. Cf. Alcoholics Anonymus, The Big Book Online (2006), 449.

35. Weil, *NFR*, 289–90. She notes how the Romans dishonored Stoicism by adopting it, but substituting prideful insensitivity for love.

36. Weil to Jöe Bousqet, 05/12/1942 (Weil, *70L*, 141).

37. Weil, *WG*, 82.

38. Weil, *WG*, 84.

39. Weil, *WG*, 89–91.

40. Weil, *WG*, 103.

41. Weil, *WG*, 104.

42. Weil, *WG*, 124.

43. Weil, *WG*, 125–6. Cf. her experience of rising above suffering to perfect joy in the beauty of religious chanting in Solesmes. (Weil, *WG*, 68).

44. Weil, *WG*, 126. Cf. Grant's description of Weil's attention as "*l'action non-aggressante.*" (Grant, "Excerpts from Graduate Lectures," *CW* 4: 827–8).

45. Weil, *WG*, 131.

46. Weil, *WG*, 132.

47. Weil, *WG*, 137.

48. "*Theaetetus*—astonishment—cf. dark night." (Weil, *NB* 1: 132).

49. Weil, "Two Poems," *SWR*, 408–9.

50. Weil, *NB* 2: 527.

51. Grant, "Excerpts from Graduate Lectures," *CW* 4: 827–8. See on "the intelligence enlightened by love" as knowledge: Hugh D. Forbes, *A Guide* (2007), 218; David Cayley, *GC*, 175–9.

52. Weil, *NB* 1: 242.

53. Weil, *G-G*, 84. Cf. Grant, "Excerpts from Graduate Lectures," *CW* 4: 827–8.

54. Eric O. Springsted, "The Attention of Awaiting God," *Paying Attention to the Sky* (2010), (citing Weil, "Reflections on the Right Use of School Studies," *WG*, 57–65).

55. Weil, *NB* 1: 179.

56. Weil, *NB* 1: 205.

57. Weil, *NB* 1: 215.

58. Weil, *NB* 1: 272.

59. Plato, *Letters* (1966), 7:341c–d. Cf. 344c.

60. Cf. Michael Ross, "Transcendence, Immanence, and Practical Deliberation," *The Christian Platonism of Simone Weil* (2004), 49.

61. Weil, *WG*, 57.

62. Weil, *NB* 1: 215.

63. Weil, *SNL*, 118–20. Italics are in the original to denote Plato's words or Weil's emphasis.

64. Plato, *The Republic* 6.493c.

65. Weil, *IC*, 75.

66. Cf. esp. her identification of 'Pythagorean harmony' incarnated in the crucified just man (*Republic*) and crucified World Soul (*Timaeus*).

Gabellieri, "Reconstructing Platonism" (2004), 141.

67. Emmanuel Gabellieri, "Reconstructing Platonism" (2004), 139.

68. Weil, *IC*, 196.

69. Weil, *NB* 1: 385

70. Weil, *WG*, 81.

71. See Jersak, "Beyond Dualism," *MSO*, 221–6.

72. Weil, *SNL*, 159. Cf. Weil, *NB* 2: 448–9; Weil, *WG*, 61.

73. Plato, *Phaedrus* (1925), 253a.

74. Weil, *G-G*, 65.

75. Eric O. Springsted, "I Dreamed I Saw St. Augustine ...," *The Christian Platonism of Simone Weil* (2004), 221.

76. Springsted, "I Dreamed I Saw St. Augustine" (2004), 221.

77. Weil, *NB* 1: 25.

78. Weil, *FLN*, 146.

79. Springsted, "I Dreamed I Saw St. Augustine" (2004), 223. Springsted's examples include Augustine, Dionysos, Bonaventure, Eckhart, and St. John of the Cross.

80. Weil, *SNL*, 104.

81. Grant, "Conversation: Theology and History," *GP*, 105.

82. Grant, "Faith and the Multiversity," *CW* 4: 623.

83. Grant, "The Moving Image of Eternity," *Ideas* (1986), 26–7.

84. Cf. Joan O'Donovan, *Twilight of Justice* (1984), 176; Edwin Heaven and David Heaven, "Some Influences of Simone Weil," *GP*, 73; W. R. Sheppard, "The Suffering of Love" (1990), 21.

85. Grant, "Conversation: Intellectual Background," *GP*, 65–6.

86. Grant, "Excerpts from Graduate Seminar Lectures on Simone Weil," *CW* 4: 828.

87. Cf. George Woodcock, "Review of Joan E. O'Donovan's *George*

*Grant and the Twilight of Justice,"* The Globe and Mail (1985); Sheppard, "The Suffering of Love" (1990), 27.

88. Weil to Andre Weil, 01–04/1940 (Weil, *70L*, 122).

89. Weil, *NB* 1: 199, 203, 429.

# 3

# Competing Conceptions of God in Biblical Religion

### Simone Weil: Competing conceptions of God

George Grant once said that theology takes the Christian tradition as a given, but avoids the uncertainty and wonder of philosophy.[1] For Grant, the only givens are the elemental doctrines of his own conversion. Aside from a firm commitment to the Gospels,[2] his openness to truth allows and equips him to see the taproot of modernity imbedded in profound difficulties of his own Bible.[3] Most important are the competing versions of God in the text itself, amplified for Grant by the influence of Simone Weil. Her notebooks are replete with entries narrating the disparities between the 'willing God' of omnipotent power and conquest versus the 'good God' whose humility is evident in the creation story and the Passion of Christ.[4] Grant says enough to reveal this issue and her interpretation as the linchpin to his construal of modern origins in biblical religion.

Weil could be scathing in her disdain for 'Jehovah' insofar as the text portrays Him as that former, willing God. How can we account for the heterodox liberties she takes in these attacks, for which she has been labeled a 'self-hating Jew'?

- She was a Jew, albeit a secular Jew who did not like being discriminated against for a faith she had never practiced.
- She was a Jew in the days leading up to the Nazi holocaust, before the post-war era when negativity about historic Israel or the Hebrew Scriptures was

tantamount to anti-Semitism.
- She was a Jew who could see firsthand the ethnic cleansing *of* Jews in Europe and *by* Jews in the Book of Joshua, side by side.
- She was a Jew in the tradition of the Hebrew prophets, who were supremely self-critical of idolatry and injustice within their own nation.
- She was an experimental theologian who thought aloud in journals never intended for publication. In these journals, she displays nuanced and often contradictory assertions—the raw material of her explorations.

J. Edgar Bauer asserts,

In light of these significant nuances, her approach of Judaism, far from being a token of Jewish self-hatred, is indicative of a self-critical intelligence prepared to question generally cherished assumptions for the sake of the truth it relentlessly searches. In the last resort, Simone Weil's intellectual endeavors are remindful of the anti-idolatrous, self-critical tradition that was grounded by the Hebrew prophets.[5]

Finally, she was also a Christian 'prophet' in that she held the Church's feet to the fire.[6] Her question is not whether Christians are superior to Jews. Rather, she confronts the Church for worshiping the image of the national military gods of Joshua and Julius Caesar, and abandoning the perfectly Good God and Father of Socrates and Jesus. The chauvinistic, crusading Church since Augustine fell in line with the former image. It had lost its catholicity and ceased to bear the light of good news to the broader world that she loved so dearly. Those who knew her testified,

Why did she fling herself into this adventure and allow herself to be carried away by such prejudices, such insufficient information and such unverifiable hypotheses? Mainly for two reasons: her love for those in affliction, whom she was anxious not to deprive of the presence of Christ. 'Christ is present on this earth wherever there is crime or afflictions unless men drive him away. Otherwise what would be the meaning of the mercy of God?' (*Connaissance Surnaturelle, page 36*).[7]

Grant, on the other hand, was compelled to guard his tongue, even where we detect Weil's ideas churning in his mind. He rightly restrains himself since he was not a Jew; he lived in the post-war period of Holocaust remorse; and what he produced was composed for public consumption. Propriety was expected and appropriate. He was certainly not anti-Semitic: Jesus, Weil, and Strauss (all Jews) are his greatest authorities. Yet, like Weil in his sensitivity to the horrors of war, Grant is often repulsed by what he reads in the OT. The issue is not competing religions (Judaism vs. Christianity), but two competing images of God within the Bible.

We will appraise Weil's analysis of these Gods, and then turn to the attributes Grant infers from them as kernels of modern ideology.

### The 'willing God' or 'Great Beast'

Weil regarded 'the willing God' as a self-justifying conception of totalitarian societies. The codeword she uses for social idolatry is 'the Great Beast,' described by Plato in *The Republic Book VI* and picked up in John's Apocalypse. She names it wherever she sees it, from ancient Israel and Rome to modern Marxism and America. She believed that Israel (the religious beast) and Rome (the materialist beast) corrupted Christianity with the spirit of the Beast when it was adopted as the official state religion.[8] Thus, the (Catholic) Church came to worship the Beast as an 'ersatz form of God' and so became the totalitarian Beast herself.[9] Through the doctrine of providence, the Church would purport to be a history-maker in the name of this (false) God.[10]

> The service of the false God (of the Social Beast in whatever form it may be) purifies evil by eliminating the horror of it. Nothing seems ... evil to him who serves the false God, except lapses in the performance of his service. ... Whilst one has a horror of this evil, at the same time one loves it as emanating from the will of God. ... Everything is permissible to him who is able to do everything. He who serves an All-powerful Being can do all in and through him. Force sets one free form the pair of opposites Good-Evil.[11]

### Jehovah vs. Jesus (OT vs. NT)

To Weil, the NT unequivocally represents Christ crucified as the perfect and complete image of the invisible God[12]—God is (re)defined as a gracious and forgiving Father, a hidden Father who rewards in secret[13] (Matt. 6:6). This Good God combines the universal and the particular in the harmony of incarnation[14] through a righteous young Jew who shows us supernatural love and humility on a Cross. The God of grace and mercy abdicates omnipotent force[15] and takes the form of a suffering servant who loves even his enemies.

Weil and Grant see this same humble and loving God in the OT Creation narratives and in some post-exilic prophets. But frequently, the Jewish canon appears to emphasize Jehovah as a willing God of overwhelming power and violent wrath. He manifests through a nationalist religion whose statutes call for conquest and enslavement, and through judges and prophets who command genocides in God's name—*because he can. Because he wills it.* "I am the Potter, you are the clay" (cf. Jer. 18:1–6). "I am who I am. I will be what I will be" (cf. Exod. 3:12–15). Fine, say Grant and Weil, but are you Good?

> There is this trying tension ... within Biblical Judaism, and Grant saw it most clearly. God is about justice,

peace and mercy, but he is also the Lord of war and violence. There seems to be an inconsistency in these two myths and motifs. There are moments within Biblical Judaism when both God and the Jewish people work within the framework of justice, mercy and peace, and there are may other moments when anger, wrath, war and violence dominate the day. Whose view of God should be trusted and why? Grant suggested, from a close reading of Biblical Judaism, that the Biblical God of Judaism (and the people God had chosen) set in motion a way of thinking that had serious consequences. If God could choose to will whatever He wished, how could humans truly trust such an unpredictable King and Lord?[16]

The more Christocentric one's theology, the more offensive this OT punisher-god appears—and if we are honest, he *does* appear. If, as the NT insists, the true God is *exactly* like Jesus, and *always has been* (Mal. 3:6; Heb. 13:8), then what has the Father-God of Jesus to do with Joshua or Samuel's Warrior-God (1 Sam. 15), demanding the extermination or enslavement of whole races? Thus, Weil draws a stark boundary between Jehovah's power and Jesus' refusal of power:

> Jehovah made the same promises to Israel that the Devil made to Christ. God is only all-powerful here below for saving those who desire to be saved by Him. He has abandoned all the rest of his power to the Prince of this world and to inert matter. He has no power other than spiritual.[17]

> War is the supreme form of prestige. ... That is why there is something essentially false in the Old Testament (certain parts), as also in the story of Joan of Arc: her voices are bound up with prestige. So also is Jehovah.

> However just the cause of the conqueror may be, however just that of the conquered, the evil caused, whether

by victory or by defeat, is none the less inevitable. ... That is why Christ did not come down from the Cross, and did not even remember, at the moment of supreme anguish, that he would return to life.[18]

'We believe by tradition in the case of the gods, and we see by experience in the case of men, that always, through a necessity of nature, everything exercises all the power at his disposal.' This is not true of the God of the Christians. He is a *supernatural* God, whereas Jehovah is a *natural* God.[19]

Of course, Weil and Grant were not the first to notice the problem. After a period of emphasizing the continuity of the Hebrew Scriptures and the Gospel as promise-fulfillment, the early church had to face these serious elements of discontinuity between Christ and Yahweh—they fought and even split over it.

Early options included abandoning the Old Testament (Marcion); others saw distinct gods and/or 'demiurges' within the OT (Valentinus); while others settled on allegorizing the conquest texts (Origen).[20] What all agreed on (until Augustine's 'just war theory') was that Christ's revelation of God as love unveiled genuine problems with (parts of) the Hebrew revelation of Yahweh.

Weil anticipates the argument from 'mystery.' Perhaps the love of God and the violence of God are compatible in a realm beyond finite understanding? Normally Weil embraced contraries, but now she says, No! Here we have a genuine contradiction. If the willful God of the OT is a mystery, then two types of mystery exist: The mysteries of the true God (e.g., the Incarnation, the Eucharist) project light. The mysteries of divine genocide project only darkness.[21] They are of a different spirit. Recall this Gospel pericope:

And [Jesus] sent messengers ahead of him, who went and entered a village of the Samaritans, to make preparations for him. But the people did not receive him, because his face was set toward Jerusalem. And when his disciples James and John saw it, they said, "Lord, do you want us to tell fire to come down from heaven and consume them?" But he turned and rebuked them. (Luke 9:52–55)

Why does Jesus forbid his disciples from invoking destruction by fire? Is it because we have now entered an age of grace? Or because their day of judgment will come later? Some translations report,

> But He turned and rebuked them, [and said, "*You do not know what kind of spirit you are of;* for the Son of Man did not come to destroy men's lives, but to save them"] (Luke 9:55–56 NASB).

Is he implying that the God who once rained fire and brimstone on Sodom and Gomorrah is *not* the same spirit that he represents? The destroying God and the saving God are, at least in this passage, incompatible.[22]

## Hebrew-Roman tradition vs. Greek-Gospel tradition

How do Weil and Grant handle the Jehovah versus Jesus discrepancy? First, they broaden it to envision two wider representations of God in antiquity: the willing God of power, force, and conquest associated with Hebrew and Roman religion vis-à-vis the Good God of selfless love and grace in Plato's *Dialogues* and the Christ of the Gospels. They believed that the Western Church was polluted, not by Hellenization,[23] but by worship of the Hebrew-Roman God of conquest. By choosing this willing God, the Church inevitably spawned the modern willing man of political and technological conquest:

> Christianity became a totalitarian, conquering and destroying agent because it failed to develop the notion

of the absence and non-action of God here below. It attached itself as much to Jehovah as to Christ, and conceived of Providence after the style of the Old Testament. Israel alone was able to resist Rome, because it resembled Rome; and so it came about that the newly-born Christianity was contaminated by Rome *before* it ever became the official religion of the Empire. The evil wrought by Rome has never been truly repaired.[24]

Jehovah, the Church of the Middle Ages, H. [*hitlérisme!*]—all these are earthly Gods. The purification they effect is an imaginary one. The errors of our time are the result of Christianity minus the supernatural element. This is due to '*läicisme*' (secularization), and in the first place, to humanism.[25]

### The powerless creator vs. mighty conqueror

This is not to say that Weil rejected the God of the OT *en toto*. Incongruous images of the Divine already appear within the Hebrew canon. At times Yahweh is Israel's faithful Romancer, eternally patient and persistent. Alternately, he divorces them—leads armies to pillage and burn their cities, and sends survivors into exile. Sometimes Israel is God's sword of ethnic cleansing; at other times, his target for siege and obliteration. Elsewhere, He is the light of the whole world, desire of the nations, our Prince of Peace and universal blessing.

Weil works with this patchwork. She may disparage Jehovah when that name represents Israel's social idolatry. But at the same time, the 'I Am' of the Torah was, for her, the name of the true God (Exod. 3:14).[26] Weil's selectivity is not arbitrary; she holds the crucified Christ as the template over the biblical text to screen what can and cannot be received:

> Among all the books of the Old Testament, only a small number (Isaiah, Job, the Song of Solomon, Daniel,

Tobias, part of Ezekiel, part of the Psalms, part of the Book of Wisdom, the beginning of Genesis ... ) are able to be assimilated by a Christian soul, ... The rest is indigestible, because it is lacking in an essential truth which lies at the heart of Christianity and which the Greeks understood perfectly well—namely, the possibility of the innocent suffering affliction.

... One may lay down a postulate: All conceptions of God which are incompatible with a movement of pure charity are false.[27]

She also describes Isaiah the prophet as the first to bring 'de la lumière pure' (pure light) and testifies that his 'paroles fulgurantes' (shining words) about the Suffering Servant urged her to believe."[28]

In her *Notebooks*, Weil repeatedly affirms the humility, suffering, and charity of the OT Creator. The true God withdrew from being everything and abdicated his 'all-powerfulness' to make space for creation, for us, and even for suffering and evil.[29] *Divine love put limits on divine power*, deferring to creatures who prefer themselves to God, and so suffering in both Creation and the Passion.[30] For Weil, creation is God's crucifixion, something eternal.[31] By retreating from intervention, God empties himself and hides, chaining himself to necessity from the beginning.[32] Thus he is the Lamb slain, not only on the Cross, but from the foundation of the world (Rev. 13:8).[33] This God absences himself and renounces force, yet remains present in the beauty of creation and the goodness of people whose hearts bear supernatural love.[34]

For Weil, "the false God changes suffering into violence; the true God changes violence into suffering."[35] "But everything I suffer, God suffers it too, for that is the effect produced by necessity, the free play of which he refrains from violating."[36]

### Weil's two faces of God: Dual causality

Weil supplants these contradictory images of God (the omnipotent willing God versus the good and loving God) with her version of Plato's dual causality.[37] The real dilemma, for Weil, is that God is simultaneously the author of all that is *and* only that which is good.[38] Her solution is to transpose Plato's dual causality of Reason and Necessity (*Timaeus* 48a) into two faces of God: (i) *love* or grace, as God the Son, the eternal self-renouncing sacrificial Lamb[39] and (ii) *necessity* or gravity, as God the Father's created order of mechanical secondary causes. The distance between necessity and the Good in Plato thus becomes the distance between God the Father and God the Son in Weil, bridged by the Cross.[40]

She then offers this hermeneutical key: 'power' is always a *metaphor for necessity* or natural and supernatural consequences rather than a direct act of miraculous intervention. Thus, the 'power of God' (whether in wrath or deliverance) in the Bible is an existential description of secondary causes. The reality, she says, is that God is impartial (i.e., "God causes the rain to fall on the just and the unjust" or "Zeus's golden scales"[41]). 'Force' as we experience it is the mechanism (necessity) of the world (like gravity[42])—not arbitrary intervention. Beyond that, force is evil, because it is the opposite of love, which is consent.[43] So Grant understood her:

> In some Christian theological speculation the Creation and the Passion are opposed to each other, but to SW they are finally one. Now clearly this fundamental humility is a radical contrast with the image of God we have as power: *Rex tremendae majestatis* (*Dies irae*). How do we put together this humility of God with His power? His abdication of power? Does not power conflict with love? According to SW the true sense of the *metaphor of power* is that when we understand it, we know that *power as necessity*.

Thus in her writing the two different faces which God presents to us are presented as two different causalities, the necessary and the good.[44]

**Bare monotheism vs. Trinitarian-polytheist mediator**

A final essential in Weil and Grant's wariness of the OT God is the 'bare monotheism' of Israel. Most Bible students fairly assume the OT Yahweh is intended to correlate to the Christian Trinity while the Roman gods are parallel versions of the Greek pantheon, but Weil and Grant (and Nietzsche) dare to redraw the boundaries.

a. *Plato's 'God'*: First, while Socrates paid tribute to the gods (*The Republic* 1.1), he also resisted their bad character and advised censoring passages in Homer where their poor example would corrupt childhood education (*The Republic*, 3). Plato's Socrates can arguably practice polytheism *or* be accused of atheism (*The Apology*), but at the height of his theology (according to Grant and Weil, certainly)[45] Plato points to one ultimate, transcendent Good (i.e., God), the 'author and composer of the world,' the cause of all that is good (*Timaeus* 28–30, 36), and 'measure of all things' (*Laws* 4.716c). To Grant and Weil, Plato's Good/God aligned with the character of the NT 'Father.'

b. *Plato's 'Trinity'*: Second, Weil compulsively experiments with various Trinitarian models.[46] In Plato, she cites the Good, the Beautiful, and the Necessary; or Creator, Inspirer, and Mediator; or the Good, the Necessary, and the Mediator between the two.[47] She finds the Trinity again in *Parminides*: "The One qua One doesn't exist—God only as purely One is God under the aspect of non-being, of a vacuum. God *qua* being is three ( ... and why limit oneself to three, yet there must be a reason)."[48] Thus she sees greater commonality in the Christian Trinity to the Greeks than she would with the monotheism of Judaism (and Rome and Islam[49]).

c. *'Incarnations and Mediators'*: To Weil, a trinity is crucial because it supplies a *mediator* to bridge the distance between God and the world, time and eternity, necessity and the Good.[50] And a Trinity provides an *incarnation* through which the goodness of the transcendent may graciously enter the world. The Mediator may be Love, Beauty, Christ, Prometheus, Osiris, Dionysus, Krishna, or Melchizedek.[51] Regardless, she says, "The Trinity is *indispensable* to the Greek and Christian notion of justice."[52] Why?

d. *The Danger of 'Bare monotheism'*: Weil's theorizes that when monotheistic religion has no mediator, the sword—aggressive national destiny—becomes your mediator:

> Moses, Joshua, Samuel. The point at issue was to forge, without a conception of the Incarnation, a whole monotheistic people, thinking on God in His entirety, without an intermediary. ... For want of a μεταξύ (*metaxu*), the sword played the part of μεταξύ; terror and expectation, horrible and bloody deeds, and the flowing of milk and honey. There was no possibility of its being otherwise.[53]

Weil judges the monotheism of Israel, Imperial Rome, and now Islam, as the ignorance and rejection of Incarnation, a darkening of hearts that always slips from true universal monotheism into faith in a tribal deity who incarnates as national exceptionalism:

> There cannot be any contact as from one person to another between man and God except through the person of the Mediator. Apart from him, the only way in which God can be present to man is in a collective, a national way. Israel, at the same time, and at one stroke, chose the national God and rejected the Mediator. It is possible that Israel may from time to time have sought after a genuine monotheism. But it always fell back upon, the tribal God.[54]

On the potential violence of monotheism sans mediator,

Grant is pure Weilian:

> There is in Islam and Judaism this bare monotheism, which makes me hesitant about their accounts of polytheism. It's very strange that Islam and Judaism should be politically at war now because I find in both of them the same thing, something I am frightened of, the overwhelming power of this very bare monotheism.[55]

Grant, more careful with his language, left Weil to risking provocative associations between Jehovah, the Crusades, and Hitler. But he did quietly make the case for a Christianity more 'Eastern,' more universal and more inclusive:

> I do not like talking in public these days of the difference between Judaism and Christianity. I don't think any political good is served by talking of such differences, ... But that does not mean there aren't grave intellectual differences between Christianity and Judaism. Clearly, for myself, I'm on the side of Christianity that is farthest away from Judaism, and nearest to the account of Christianity that is close to Hinduism in its philosophical expression. I would accept what Clement of Alexandria said: some were led to the Gospel by the Old Testament, many were led by Greek philosophy. ... What I would object to in many modern theologians (particularly the Germans) is that they make Christianity depend on the religious history of a particular people, as told in the Old Testament. They make Christianity such a "historical" religion that its universal teaching about perfection and affliction is lost.[56]

Why did Grant resist anchoring Christianity in Jewish history as the Western Church had done? Had he watered down Christian faith to a 'pale Hellenism'? No, he explains, his battle is with the Church's use of the Bible to construct the image of God as dynamic power and arbitrary will—the same traits modernity adopted to make God expendable.

Obviously there are wonderful and true things in the Old Testament. There are also exclusivist parts. What I want to insist is that the universal truth of Christ is not tied to an account of God's *dynamic activity* in the world, which appears to me to be unthinkable and to *lead directly to atheism*. Both western accounts of Christianity—Protestant and Catholic—have emphasized the *arbitrary power* of God in a way which seems to me fundamentally wrong and which has produced a picture of a God whom one should not worship. I think those emphases on the power of God are related to that *exclusivity and dynamism* which have led to some of the worst sides of western civilization. We in the West are called to rethink all this, which started somewhere close to St Augustine. What seems to me sad is that just when this rethinking is so necessary, many theologians are reemphasizing this God of dynamism in the name of the Bible.[57]

## Critique

Grant and Weil's presentation of the biblical God is vulnerable to critique. Briefly, whenever they refer to God's active work in history, they don the lens of nationalist conquest under a King who rules with a rod of iron. That theme is prevalent in the Bible, but so too are the prophets' hopes for a Deliverer from exile and a Restorer of justice and peace. Isaiah and company foresee Israel's election as a chosen herald of blessing to the world, a beacon of light with universal good news. Moreover, Israel's deliverance is prophesied as Yahweh's personal visitation to Israel, embodied in a messianic mediator,[58] whose deliverance is achieved through suffering (cf. Isaiah 42–53). The prophetic warnings are not reducible to Zionist sabre-rattling, but start with indictments of Jerusalem. The criterion for judgment is whether she has fulfilled her calling and been merciful and just to widows, orphans, and strangers (i.e., immigrants).

Most importantly, the Jesus of the Gospels was undoubtedly a Jewish prophet who embraced Israel's core beliefs: monotheism, election, and eschatology. He believed that Yahweh would act in history to deliver humankind from spiritual darkness, and that he would embody that salvation through his own climactic career.[59] At some point, one would expect Christocentric believers like Weil and Grant to bow to Jesus' theology of God the Redeemer.

We might ask whether the real offence for Grant and Weil was not also God's *lack* of intervention in their time. Where was the God 'who is able to deliver' for the Jews of Europe now? Had Yahweh evaporated in Hitler's ovens? To their credit, they looked for God in God's perceived absence, as the crucified Christ suffering with the afflicted once again. But is that really the final hope of the Jewish or Christian God? Grant and Weil were prejudiced against identifying God with victory (even in the resurrection) because they saw how triumphalism served the propaganda of empires. But in so doing, they are forerunners in idealizing 'the weakness of God' (*a la* Dietrich Bonhoeffer to John Caputo). But does such an impotent deity deserve the 'God' label? In what sense does this God 'care'? How can their God be called 'Saviour'? Can such a God even be said to exist? Thus, S. A. Taubes dubs Weil's theology 'religious atheism':

> When Neitzsche (sic) announced that God is dead, he planted the seed for a new kind of atheism ... Religious atheism ... invests the natural world, from which divine presence and providence have been totally excluded, with theological significance. ... The thesis of religious atheism has been most boldly formulated by Simone Weil: the existence of God may be denied without denying God's reality. ... The mortification of God in the world becomes the theological starting point for the life of the spirit in God.[60]

Taubes surely overstates her case—for Weil faithfully extends the agnostic theology of the apophatic mystics (Simeon the New Theologian, 949–1042) and St. John of the Cross (1542–1591). Yes, her God is absent in the sense of intervention or providence, but very much present in the supernatural compassion of His people:

> God is absent from the world except in the existence in this world of those in whom His love is alive. ... Their compassion is the visible presence of God here below. ... Through compassion we can put the created, temporal part of a creature in communication with God. ... Compassion is what spans the abyss which creation has open between God and the creature. It is the rainbow.[61]

That said, and to conclude, Weil made this much clear to Grant:

- The Bible itself presents genuinely contradictory images of God.
- The Western Church had chosen to worship *and embody* the willful and triumphalistic God.
- In its liberation from the Church, the West nevertheless became the willful and triumphalistic society of modernity.
- Such a society will implode ethically because its foundations are built on the sand of self-will.

## Endnotes

1. Grant, "George Grant and Religion: Conversation with William Christian," *CW* 4: 745.

2. Grant, "Conversation," *GC*, 108.

3. Cf. Simone Weil: "Christ likes us to prefer truth to him because, before being Christ, he is truth. If one turns aside from him to go toward the truth, one will not go far before falling into his arms." (WG, 69).

4. Weil, *Pensées*, 48.

5. J. Edgar Bauer, "Simone Weil: Kenotic Thought and 'Sainteté Nouvelle,'" *Center for Studies on New Religions Conference* (2002).

6. Cf. Weil, *LP*, 26–9, where her agenda is to resist the corruption behind Church's exclusive claims, historic atrocities, and contribution to progressivism.

7. Joseph Marie Perrin, et al., *Simone Weil as We Knew Her* (2003), 60.

8. Weil, *FLN*, 120, 304–5; *NB* 2: 482.

9. Weil, *NB* 2: 618.

10. Weil, *NB* 2: 380, 620.

11. Weil, *NB* 2: 504–5. Cf. Weil, *FLN*, 124–5.

12. John 1:1, 14; Col. 1:15, 2:9; Heb. 1:3; 2 Cor. 5:19.

13. Weil, *FLN*, 259–60, 275.

14. Weil, *FLN*, 286.

15. God is only all-powerful indirectly, abdicating his will to necessity. "Love is abdication. God is abdication." (Weil, *FLN*, 103, 296–300).

16. Ron Dart, *George Grant: Spiders and Bees* (2008), 148.

17. Weil, *FLN*, 100.

18. Weil, *NB* 1: 25. Cf. Weil, *NFR*, 96–7.

19. Weil, *NB* 1: 190.

20. Hence Weil's interest in early Gnostics, such as Valentinus and Marcion, and her reputation for so-called Gnostic Anti-Judaism. Cf. Sylvie Courtine-Denamy, et al., *Three Women in Dark Times: Edith Stein, Hannah Arendt, Simone Weil* (2000), 143–6.

21. Weil, *NB* 2: 454.

22. This ignores the many judgment parables in the Gospels, where God is portrayed as the returning King who, through Rome, destroys the rebellious city and its corrupted temple. Yet these imply indirect consequences, not direct intervention.

23. As in Adolf von Harnack's model. Cf. Pope Benedict XVI, "Three Stages in the Program of De-Hellenization," *Papal Address at the University of Regensburg* (2006).

24. Weil, *NB* 2: 505, 571.

25. Weil, *NB* 2: 502.

26. "Dieu seul a le droit de dire 'Je suis'; 'Je suis' est son nom et n´est le nom d´aucun autre être." ("God alone has the right to say 'I am'; 'I am' is his name and is the name of no other being.") (Weil, IC, 137). Compare to, "The Great Beast's end is existence. 'I am that I am.'" (Weil, *NB* 2: 620).

27. Weil, *LP*, 41. Cf. 26. She surmises that these books must have been imported from Chaldean or Egyptian religion, who knew of a mediating, suffering and redemptive God (48).

28. Bauer, "Kenotic Thought.'" *New Religions Conference* (2002).

29. Note the similarities to the *tzimtzum* of the Lurianic Kabbalah—where Jewish Kabbalism intersects with Platonism and Gnosticism.

30. Weil, *NB* 2: 507, 560.

31. Weil, *NB* 2: 400, 564.

32. Weil, *NB* 1: 191–3.

33. Weil, *NB* 1: 222, 246; 2: 380, 536, 538, 564.

34. Weil, *NB* 1: 317; 2: 358, 403.

35. Weil, *NB* 2: 507.

36. Weil, *NB* 1: 191.

37. Miklós Vetö, *The Religious Metaphysics of Simone Weil* (1994), 12–13.

38. Weil, *NB* 1: 207; 2: 352.

39. Weil, *NB* 2: 564.

40. Weil, *NB* 2: 400, 428, 557

41. Weil, *NB* 1: 221.

42. Weil, *NB* 1: 71, 74; 2: 499.

43. Weil, *NB* 2: 450, 476, 492.

44. Grant, "Excerpts from Graduate Seminar Lectures," *CW* 4: 822.

45. E.g., Weil, *IC*.

46. Including her meditations on Hinduism: God as Brahma (preserver) as the Word, Vishnu (creator) as the Father, and Shiva (destroyer, de-creator) as the Spirit (Weil, *NB* 1: 264–5).

47. Weil, *NB* 2: 379–80.

48. Weil, *NB* 1: 319.

49. Rome, because her true religion was the monotheism of Empire; Islam, for the same reasons as Israel (*NB* 1: 261; 2: 565, 581).

50. Weil, *NB* 1: 221.

51. Weil, *NB* 2: 351. She allows for human incarnations within the OT, but Jewish tradition would disagree. However, why did the 'angel of the Lord' theophanies not meet her criteria?

52. Weil, *NB* 2: 379, 439.

53. Weil, *NB* 1: 102.

54. Weil, *NB* 2: 581. Still, she says that Israel's ignorance of incarnation was necessary so the Passion might be possible (Weil, *NB* 2: 565).

55. Cayley, *GC*, 130–1.

56. Grant, "Conversation," *GP*, 102.

57. Grant, "Conversation," *GP*, 102–3.

58. Ps. 50:3–4; 96:12–13; 98:8–9; Isa. 4:2–6; 24:23; 25:9–10; 35:3–6, 10; 40:3–5, 9–11; 52:7–10; 59:15–17, 19–21; 60:1–3; 62:10–11; 63:1, 3, 5, 9; 64:1; 66:12, 14–16, 18–19; Ezek. 43:1–7; Hag. 2:7, 9; Zech. 8:2–3; Zech 14:1–5, 9, 16; Mal. 3:1–4.

59. Cf. N. T. Wright, *Jesus and the Victory of God* (1996), 612–54.

60. Susan A. Taubes, "The Absent God," *Journal of Religion* 35 (01/1995): 6–7.

61. Weil, *FLN*, 103.

# Part 2

# George Grant:
# Red Tory

# 4

# Grant and the Matrix: Complex of Ideologies

George Grant saw modernity as the dominant, unchallenged dogma of the day, a matrix of divergent emphases (from Marxism to American Republicanism; from Rationalist to Romantic; from Luther to Nietzsche; from the Calvinist Puritans to the American Civil Liberties Association) and definitions. The following pervasive ideologies summarize this complex of ideologies as Grant saw and spoke about them.

**Progressivism**

Progressivism is Hegel's 'dialectic of history,' in which truth, freedom, and justice emerge as time progressively unfolds through the dialectic of history (which becomes a secularized doctrine of providence). Contra Hegel, Grant draws from Plato's eternal order of knowing and being that transcends history: "The moving image of eternity."[1] Living in alignment with the eternal good results in true freedom and justice. (Summary: eternity versus progress).

**Liberalism**

Liberalism, for Grant, is freedom defined as our human essence to shape the world as we want it, or as 'the will to power.' Grant assesses a variety of liberal streams, defined as he sees them as seeking freedom through the control of human and non-human nature. He tracks human 'willing' through:

- freedom as individualism or voluntarism (Luther to Nietzsche);

- freedom as equality (whether Marxist or American liberalism): Grant's Yes to Nietzsche;
- freedom through contractualism (Rousseau to Rawls); and
- freedom by pragmatism (Calvinist Puritans to American Imperialism).

Nietzsche helps Grant detect the modernist will to power vis-à-vis the subordination of the will to the Good (though Nietzsche exalts that which he exposes—and in this sense, is for Grant an uber-modern). Grant draws from Plato and Weil to proclaim a different kind of freedom that depends on allowing 'the eternal world of truth and goodness' to rule our thoughts and actions[2] through charity. (Summary: the Good versus freedom.)

**Technological mastery**

Technological mastery is, for moderns, the way of freedom. Grant critiques the western way of knowing and being that shapes its own destiny through technological mastery. He challenges science's claims to objective, values-free education and technology (judging by its sketchy ethical fruit) and draws from Heidegger and Weil to revive interest in classical openness to being and meaning. Heidegger helps Grant see the way technology erodes our capacity for contemplative thinking, but parts from him over where to direct that openness. (Summary: mastery versus openness).

**Historicism**

Historicism is 'time as history.' Heidegger saw Being in Time apart from transcendence, our need to heed our emergent being contemplatively here and now. Nietzsche too called us to accept 'the finality of becoming.'[3] For some, this sounds like absolute freedom and opportunity, an existential invitation to live courageously in the world. But for Grant, Platonist as he was, he sensed 'intimations of deprival,' that historicism tethers us too tightly to the subjectivity of the present moment. Rather, he believed in the eternal as primary and that history derives meaning from that which is permanent. He believed it was possible to remember, to think, and to love a Good/God within the details of our particular fates. (Summary: time as history versus eternity as primary).

**Rationalism/Empiricism**

Rationalism/empiricism can be equated with excluded knowledge. Finally, Grant also challenged modernity's inevitable enthronement of rational and empirical knowledge to the exclusion of contemplative knowledge. The cumulative consequences of Descartes' or Kant's delimiting the outer limits of rational or practical knowledge are that eventually, rational and empirical knowledge become the limits of knowledge (this is all we can know) and finally, we are left with a radically immanentist reality (this is all there is). Marry that to the Baconian use of scientific knowledge for the purpose of mastery and the point or even possibility of contemplative knowing is subordinated and finally dismissed with prejudice. With no sense of the transcendent—if freedom through mastery is the pinnacle of human enlightenment—what foundation is there for justice? Grant examined the philosophers who took this question seriously (from Kant to Rousseau to Rawls) and calls us back to the Good of Plato and the Love of Christ. (Summary: excluded knowledge versus noetic knowledge).

One of Grant's summaries of the modernist matrix reads as follows:

> The mastery of human and non-human nature in experimental science and technique, the primacy of the will, man as the creator of his own values, the finality of becoming, the assertion that potentiality is higher than actuality, that motion is nobler than rest, that dynamism rather than peace is the height.[4]

To Grant, modern liberalism as the new establishment is found wanting in light of (i) history's tragedies and (ii) philosophy's inadequacy when judged by the standard of justice. A philosophy that cannot account for (in fact, sets up) horrendous tragedy and offers no just solution suggests we need to look elsewhere. Grant, of course, looks to Plato, Christ, Strauss, and Weil for his account of classical justice.

**Endnotes**

1. Plato, *Timaeus* 37c–e.

2. Grant, "The Minds of Men in the Atomic Age," *CW* 2: 159.

3. Cf. Grant, *TH*, 25–7.

4. Grant, *TH*, 44.

# 5

# Grant and the Matrix: Dialogue Partners

Besides composing his own definitions of modernity around freedom as willing and making, George Grant appropriates keys in dialogue with his primary guides and nemeses, depending on which element he wishes to deconstruct. One could outline his dissection of modernity by its major players and what their names symbolized to Grant.[1] Instead, I will briefly demonstrate how Grant reinforces his own sense of modernism (as a 'philosophy of will') in reaction to and interaction with five great thinkers: Georg Hegel, Leo Strauss, Martin Heidegger, Friedrich Nietzsche, and Simone Weil.

## Georg Hegel

In the first decades of Grant's career, he thought much about Georg Hegel's influence on his family and on his own worldview. When assessing the divergence of moral philosophy between the ancients and moderns—*serving* versus *shaping*—Grant analyzes and finally abandons Hegel's synthesis:

> To put this issue simply are we truly and finally *responsible for shaping what happens in the world*, or do we live in an order for which we are not ultimately responsible, so that the purpose of our lives is to discover and serve that order? There are philosophers (Hegel, for instance) who have claimed to include the truth of both these sides in their philosophies ... what matters first is to see how divergent are these ways of looking at the world and what different moralities they must lead to.[2]

### Leo Strauss

When he boils down "the modern concentration of man as historical,"[3] the contradictions in Hegel's 'progressivist vision,' or the 'lowering of sights' in Hobbes and Locke, Grant shamelessly recapitulates Leo Strauss, who opened his eyes to modernity's sacrifice of the eternal "in its attempt to become the master and possessor of nature."[4]

> The end of life, in [Hobbes and Locke] becomes comfortable self-preservation. The end of life in the ancients, the height of life, was openness to the whole, and in that openness, to know the highest good, which is God. Strauss somewhere says that the desire to overcome chance, which is in modern science and then modern political science, was probably the reason why modern human beings became oblivious to eternity.[5]

### Martin Heidegger

In our passion to make and control our destinies, Grant turns to Martin Heidegger, who revealed for him the essential link between modernity and technology as a perilous way of thinking and being. But Heidegger also showed him the possibility that "where danger is, grows there the saving power also:"[6]

> I mean by modernity the society that has come to be … since western people have concentrated on what is best called "technology." … Technology puts together what the Greeks could not possibly have put together, making and knowing. … It seems to me that modernity comes forth, above all, from this new union of the arts and sciences, and what it portends for us. … at its heart is this new interdependence of the arts and sciences—"technology." … The deepest account of modernity is found in the writings of Heidegger.[7]

## Friedrich Nietzsche

For the correspondence between modernity, mastery, and willing, he also turns to the 'great seer of the modern fate,' Friedrich Nietzsche. Nietzsche's scathing indictments against Hegelian naivety ring true to Grant and he could bear direct witness to Nietzsche's chilling visions of nihilism. Grant acknowledges that Nietzsche's thought "doesn't invent the situation of our contemporary existence, it unfolds it."[8] But in so doing, Grant senses Nietzsche only directs us deeper into the cave.

> In [Nietzsche's] work [thinking the modern project], the themes that must be thought in thinking time as history are raised to a beautiful explicitness: the mastery of human and non-human nature in experimental science and technique, the primacy of the will, man as the creator of his own values, the finality of becoming, the assertion that potentiality is higher than actuality, that motion is nobler than rest, that dynamism rather than peace is the height.[9]

## Simone Weil

Finally, Grant meets Simone Weil's thought for a "prodigious turning around from the modern at just its central point." Namely,

> The importance of Simone Weil is her attempt to express the truth of Christianity outside *the philosophy of will*.
>
> But that is prodigiously difficult to follow because (i) we are all raised with the enormous thing which is Western civilization, and that civilization at every point is expressing *truth as will*. Therefore we must recognize the extremity and root and broadness of what she is saying. (ii) We are unlikely to have her genius or her experience. I think the details of her life [express] that turn away from will as ultimate truth.[10]

So, in Grant's synthesis of these (and other) pundits, he recognizes the recurring theme central to modernity: *will as ultimate truth*. And Weil is the great renouncer of personal will[11] (to a fault). She sees the cave as the domain of the willing *"I"*[12] and strives continuously for a decreation of self. 'Nakedness of spirit' (*nudité d'esprit*[13]) prepares us for regeneration in which we recapitulate Christ's *kenosis* (self-emptying), expressed acutely in Gethsemane as, "Not my will, but thine be done,"—her anti-Nietzschean version of *amor fati*.[14] The composite self ("I," "me") dies and the uncreated self (identical with Christ) emerges.[15] A new being or "new I" is born of the seed of God—"I no longer live, but Christ lives within me" (Gal. 2:20) and through me. I imitate God's humility by withdrawing to allow space for the other: for Christ in me and for others ethically.

By renouncing the self-absorbed 'I' (*le moi*), and especially by enduring unconsoled affliction like Christ on the Cross ("My God, my God …"), a void (*le vide*) opens for God's grace and love to pass into us and through us into the world to restore justice. There, God's grace descends to enlighten our thoughts and actions with truth and goodness—a transformation undergone by any who ask for it, not by willed action.[16] Typically extreme, but true to her experience, the journey is marked by contradiction: God's goodness and our affliction—the way of the Cross.

> The ideal of justice is to be naked and dead. The Cross alone is not exposed to an imaginary imitation. So that we may feel the distance between us and God, God has to be a crucified slave. … It is not by eating of a certain tree, as Adam thought, that one becomes equal to God, but by going the way of the Cross.[17]

Not very appealing, yet is she not plainly echoing the Christ of the Gospels? Jesus said,

> Whoever wants to be my disciple must deny themselves and take up their cross daily and follow me. For

whoever wants to save their life will lose it, but whoever loses their life for me will save it. What good is it for someone to gain the whole world, and yet lose or forfeit their very self? (Luke 9:23–25 NIV)

The trouble with modernity (or simply humanity?) is that in our social and personal spheres, we would rather fill, plug, or numb the void with fantasies of a grandiose destiny.[18] Weil warns that this is a dead end, because vain imaginations serve only to close the door to grace. For Weil, modern civilization has abandoned the tradition (defined as 'desire for the Good') in exchange for the desire to "create oneself by one's actions."[19] The result over time is chronic uprootedness—expressed in wartime France as an apathetic stupor and in Germany as violent aggression. Far from enlightening us, the modern philosophy of will creates "a screen between oneself and reality."[20] 'Freedom of will,' as she saw it, involves a kind of 'stupid ... stiffening pride' vis-à-vis the 'freedom of grace' marked by attention, faith, and love.[21] She equates the 'will to power' with the Hindu Rajas[22] and the temptation of both Adam and Christ,[23] which is to say, *freedom as leaving God's path/will for your own.*

These, then, were Grant's primary interlocutors along the way. Each would appear either explicitly or implicitly in all of Grant's books, whether he was fleeing from Hegel, weeding through Nietzsche and Heidegger, or borrowing liberally from Strauss and Weil. In each case, his dialogue partners clarify the nature of modernity with increasing clarity, sharpening Grant's attack on the Matrix from within and without.

### Endnotes

1. In *We Are Not Our Own*, I expand on Grant's definition of modernity according to its major embodiments in order to include critical names and ideas that otherwise go unmentioned.

2. Grant, *PMA*, 36.

3. Grant, *TH*, 10.

4. Michael Gillespie, "George Grant and the Tradition of Political Philosophy," *By Loving Our Own* (1990), 129.

5. Cayley, *GC*, 74.

6. Martin Heidegger, "The Question Concerning Technology" (1977). Grant spent entire semesters studying this essay with his students.

7. Grant, "Conversation," *GC*, 141.

8. Grant, *TH*, 24–5.

9. Grant, *TH*, 57.

10. Grant, "Excerpts from Graduate Lectures on Simone Weil, 1975–6," *CW* 4: 833.

11. Weil, *NB* 1: 258–9.

12. Weil, *NB* 2: 349. Cf. *NB* 2: 419: "The 'I'—this is only the shadow cast by sin and error which obstruct the light coming from God, and which I take to be a being." Note how Weil's use of the 'self' or 'I' delineates 'the false self' (of pride or prestige, etc.) from 'the true self' (Christ in me) to be given in love.

13. Cp. Jesus' 'poverty of spirit' in the Beatitudes of Matt. 5.

14. Weil, *NB* 1: 38, 181.

15. Weil, *FLN*, 283, 287.

16. Weil, *NB* 1: 273, 280; 2: 411–2. Desiring and asking are the sole requirements for regeneration. She thus avoids the irresistible grace of Calvin's election *and* the 'whosoever will' voluntarism of Evangelicals (Weil, *FLN*, 290–1).

17. Weil, *NB* 2: 411, 414.

18. Weil, *G&G*, 16–17.

19. Weil, *NFR*, 48–9.

20. Weil, *NB* 1: 46.

21. Weil, *NB* 1: 205.

22. For Weil's understanding of Rajas, she quotes the Gita: "Rajas is of the nature of passion, giving rise to thirst and attachment; it binds fast by attachment to action. ... the fruit of Rajas is pain." (*NB* 1: 92).

23. Weil, *NB* 1: 270. Cf. Grant on Dostoevsky's *Grand Inquisitor.*

# 6

# Finding His Voice: Conversion to *Lament*

Following his wartime conversion,[1] George Grant emerged as a man of faith in search of understanding. His recovery period, his first teaching post at Dalhousie, and his return to Oxford to pursue a theology degree provided Grant with a chance to read and study the great minds who could give words and content to his experience. This stage of Grant's biography especially shows us how he began to construct his contemplative Christian Platonism and [anti-]theodicy of the Cross. We can observe his post-conversion development to his emergence as Canada's top philosopher (with the publication of *Lament for a Nation*) by noting those with whom he resonated, how they addressed his newfound convictions and answered his pressing questions.

**Recovery**

Regardless of his newfound faith, Grant still needed a period of physical and emotional recovery. Sudden new thoughts of hope do not usually heal TB or PTSD overnight. In February 1942, he returned to Canada where Maude could nurse him back to a measure of health. He got involved as an educator with the CAAE (Canadian Association of Adult Education) and published a few articles.[2] When the war ended, Grant opted to return to Oxford to begin a D. Phil. in theology (Oct. 1945). In 1947 he married Sheila Allen in London, a remarkable woman who not only bore him six children, but a Cambridge scholar (and student of J. R. R. Tolkien) in her own right. She researched, edited, and virtually co-wrote everything he published.³

George interrupted his studies to move back to Canada with the intention of teaching at the University of Toronto, but lost the posting when the powers that be discovered he was a pacifist and a socialist. Then a door opened at Dalhousie University in Halifax, NS where he started teaching philosophy. This brief period was foundational for two reasons. First, Grant gained a clear sense of the challenge of teaching in a Canadian university. The students and school were resistant to hearing Grant's faith-based message, even though they were very much in need of it in their post-war bewilderment. Second, he worked alongside the Hegelian philosopher, James Doull. Grant credits Doull with leading him into western philosophy, especially Plato and Kant, in a way that Grant could truly understand and teach the material. Grant asserts, "He enabled me to read Plato, and that taught me how it was possible to think rationally about God and about justice and about the things that concern us here below."⁴ "He showed me what the image of the sun in Plato's *Republic* meant. Everything that I had been trying to think came together."⁵ Essentially, both men worked to "situate Plato in relation to modernity."⁶

There, in 1949–50, Grant felt compelled to return to Oxford to complete his degree.

### Oxford: Touchstones of faith and philosophy

Oxford gave Grant a perfect milieu in which to bring his questions, to listen for intimations that would inform his experiences, and to flesh out his premises. He was accepted among his peers as a Christian, a pacifist, a lover of poetry, the classics, and especially Plato.⁷

*i. C. S. Lewis and the Socratic Club:* Among the touchstones of his faith and philosophy during this period included lecturers such as C. S. Lewis and Austin Farrer, and gatherings of the Origen Society and the Socratic Club.⁸ A keen interest and expertise existed among these circles concerning issues dear to

Grant—they helped him formulate his questions about the relationship between God, man, and nature. They thought deeply about apologetics, and, like Plato, Kant, and Hegel before them, tackled theodicy head on, not merely as rationalists but as practitioners of philosophical theology and 'contemplative theodicy.'[9] They had an enormous impact on Grant's philosophy.

*ii. Austin Farrer:* Austin Farrer, for example, astounded Grant when he first discovered him teaching on Descartes. Grant listened to his lectures at every opportunity thereafter.[10] An Anglican priest (confessor to Lewis) and Oxford lecturer, Farrer demonstrated a learned articulation of philosophy alongside an intelligent faith. He modeled an approach to integrating Athens and Jerusalem that would become Grant's hallmark.[11] He was also Grant's primary thesis examiner, an anticlimactic affair that lasted all of ten minutes.[12]

*iii. A. D. Lindsay:* A. D. Lindsay, Master of Balliol College, was also cited as Grant's greatest Oxford teacher.[13] Lindsay had previously convinced Grant of the need to stay and serve in England when the war began, even if that meant alternative service with the ambulance service.[14] Perhaps Lindsay's greatest influence was his part in finally swaying Grant from the Christian or moral pacifism he had maintained up until 1941. After the war, we see Grant adopting Lindsay's internationalism—force as a very reluctant last resort—a stance he would maintain until the fall of Diefenbaker. At that point, nuclear warheads were introduced into Canada and in his moral outrage, Grant concluded that "the use of modern weapons are 'intrinsically wicked' for the Christian."[15]

*iv. John Oman thesis:* When they reconnected at Oxford in 1945, Lindsay recommended writing a thesis[16] on John Oman, a Scottish theologian (1860–1939). Grant agreed, seeing it as an opportunity to dive into reading Plato, Aristotle, Thomas, Luther, Calvin, Descartes, Marx, Freud, and Pascal for several years.[17] Although Grant later downplayed the importance of his thesis, it provided a case study through which to ask his questions and develop his doctrine. It also allows us to overhear him working out the earliest version of his theodicy of the Cross in his affirmations and critiques of Oman.

Over the course of Grant's lifelong struggle with modernity, he discerns elements of modernity that he still held unawares in these early days. His thesis was only a modest beginning in the struggle to extricate himself from Hegel, to move beyond Kant and eventually see Nietzsche behind the language of values. He already knew by experience what Oman was about in challenging the adequacy of scientific rationalism, and preaching our dependence on, and immediate experience of, the supernatural.[18] Thus, Grant's greatest and enduring convictions—those of his conversion—already permeate the pages of his thesis. For example:

| Grant's Thesis | Grant's Doctrine |
| --- | --- |
| i. *Critique of modernity.* Bacon and Locke's empiricism, Hegel's historicism, control over nature, and the failure of liberalism in the face of war.[19] | i. *Naming the darkness as darkness—Grant's deconstruction:* The matrix of modernity. |
| ii. *Illumination of the soul by the Good.* God speaks to us through nature: in contemplation / awareness / apprehension (vs. science's comprehension / explanation for human utility). "Intellectual intuition."[20] | ii. *The intellect illumined by love—Grant's epistemology:* A contemplative understanding of *noetic* knowledge and the *vita contempletiva*. |

*iii. Christian Platonism.*

The platonic Good is fulfilled universally in a vision of the cross. *Theologia crucis*[21] (a la Luther) as a response to the problem of evil.

*iv. Ethical test of a philosophy.*

Oman's [and Lindsay's] liberal-Calvinist politics) in the face of moral crisis (WWI). "A practical theologian can be judged by his theology of politics."[22]

*iii. The perfection of God and the affliction of man— Grant's theology:*

a. Plato's distance between necessity and the Good
b. Theodicy of the Cross
c. Cosmology of Consent

*iv. The love of justice as light in the darkness—Grant's ethics:*
His politics of justice and consent, rooted in an obligation of love for the Good and the other.

A summary example of how Grant—as contemplative theologian—embeds his conversion-truths within the thesis comes in his discussion of man's nature:

> As we try to understand man's nature, we find it is of his very essence to be gripped by Something Other than himself. The essence of that Other we find to be Love. In the consciousness of being enfolded by Love is man's peace. Yet in no sense is that enfolding something that destroys our autonomy. Freely, in our contemplation, we must reach out to that embrace.... Oman's attempt in *Grace and Personality* is that through three hundred pages he ponders upon the implication of the experience.[23]

Grant's thinly veiled autobiography, to say the least.

## Finding his voice

One of Grant's criticisms of Oman was that in trying to communicate his faith to a *scientia*-minded culture, he could have made a stronger case by being more explicit in stating his premises. Upon graduating (1950), Grant's re-engagement with the philosophical community in Canada would provide some hard lessons on this front. For the next fifteen years (1948–65), he earned many battle scars in his confrontations with Canada's philosophical Sanhedrin, centralized at the University of Toronto and directed by his nemesis, Dr. Fulton Anderson (1895–1968). Grant's unabashed Christian Platonism was derided. While he learned to speak the 'language of Athens,'[24] his unwillingness to 'play the game' kept him sharp (and tactless) enough to accumulate powerful enemies. But by 1965, his persistence ensured his own place as Canada's preeminent philosopher.

Tracking this phase of Grant's career helps us see his four doctrines at work in his first public battles. It marks the earliest outworking of his first and fourth doctrines in practice: his return to the cave as a prophetic voice critiquing the dominance of modernity, especially in public education.

I see this stage of his life as a play in six acts:

### 1. 1948: Book review of Fulton Anderson

As a thirty year old novice, still in his first years at Dalhousie, Grant ventured down the perilous path of university politics by publishing a disparaging review of F. H. Anderson's *The Philosophy of Francis Bacon*. Anderson was head of the philosophy department at University of Toronto, the real seat of power in Canadian philosophy. The review was brief and pointed: Anderson had failed to judge the limitations of Bacon, whose scientific rationalism had devalued revealed religion and set us on a course to events like Hiroshima. He concludes, "This book is a useful study of an earlier philosopher of natural science. It could have been an important one if Professor Anderson had judged how that philosophy had helped to bring us to the barrenness of today."[25]

Livid, Anderson contacted to Alex Kerr, president of Dalhousie to either censure or dismiss Grant.[26] Kerr would not comply;

Anderson would not forget.

## 2. 1951: The Massey Commission

Fast-forward three years: Grant, now Dr. Grant, was George Munro Professor of Philosophy, head of the department, at Dalhousie University. His uncle, Vincent Massey, was appointed to head a Royal Commission on National Development in the Arts, Letters, and Sciences, called "The Massey Commission." It was to include an essay reporting on the state of philosophy in English-speaking Canada, especially addressing why philosophy was not a central concern in the nation. Norman MacKenzie, president of the University of British Columbia, recommended George for the task, perhaps with a nudge from Grant's brother-in-law, Geoff Andrew.[27]

Again, Fulton Anderson was outraged that this upstart was favoured with such a prestigious duty. How could a third year professor with so little education in philosophy 'scoop' seasoned veterans like Anderson, with decades of seniority and major publications?[28] His fury would rage ten-fold when he read the paper's assessment.

Grant's approach reflected the Anglo-Catholic revival of renaissance studies exemplified by C. S. Lewis[29] and French philosopher, Étienne Gilson.[30] Like them, he indicted modern philosophical teaching for ignoring the Christian tradition. Indeed, the period from 1850–1950 marked the increasing split between theology and philosophy in Canada's public universities.[31] Philosophy focused on rational thought detached from talk of God, revelation or religious tradition. And theology had become the domain of seminaries that neglected or omitted contemplative/patristic thought. Grant's essay proposed to reintegrate a platonic-patristic synthesis that the Canadian scholarly establishment had rejected for one hundred years. Queens is cited as a chief culprit and the Pontifical Institute of Medieval Studies as a happy exception.[32]

For Grant's part, it was an opportunity to write a piece directly about Christianity, for which he said later, "I got my ass kicked thoroughly in a way that was quite expensive."[33]

The lesson he took from the forthcoming backlash was the need to write and teach more indirectly about his greatest heroes: Socrates and Christ.[34] We might glean the most from Grant's essay by watching him try the state of philosophy in Canada in the courtroom of his four doctrines.

| **The Massey Commission** | **Grant's Doctrine** |
|---|---|
| i. Critique of Canada's philosophical establishment: pragmatism, positivism, scientific technique, loss of faith, loss of the whole.[35] | *i. Naming the darkness as darkness—Grant's deconstruction:* <br> The matrix of modernity. |
| ii. The importance of philosophy as rational contemplation of the Good.[36] | *ii. The intellect illumined by love— Grant's epistemology:* <br> A contemplative understanding of *noetic* knowledge and the *vita contempletiva*. |
| iii. Judging our societies' traditions: <br> a. against our intuitions of the perfection of God[37] / the Good.[38] <br> b. seeking a faith that answers the tragedies of experience.[39] | *iii. The perfection of God and the affliction of man— Grant's theology:* <br> a. Plato's distance between necessity and the Good <br> b. Theodicy of the Cross <br> c. Cosmology of Consent |
| *iv.* Thinking sensitively about spiritual problems and modern predicaments[40] to put brakes on impetuous men of action.[41] | *iv. The love of justice as light in the darkness—Grant's ethics:* <br> His politics of justice and consent, rooted in an obligation of love for the Good and the other. |

Grant indicts Canadian philosophy by asking four major questions:

- What is the role, purpose, function, and goal of philosophy?
- How is philosophy related to and / or dependent on faith?
- What place should contemplation have in the work of philosophy?
- What should the object of contemplative philosophy be?

In other words, we are watching for Grant's contemplative theology to assert itself through his 'prophetic' diagnosis of Canadian philosophy. We needn't wait long. The opening lines—lines he would stand by and pay for—read:

> The study of philosophy is the analysis of the traditions of our society and judgment of those traditions against our varying intuitions of the perfection of God. It is the contemplation of our own and other's activity, in the hope that by understanding it better we may make it less imperfect... Philosophy was therefore encouraged as the rational form of such contemplation.[42]

For Grant, philosophy's role is to "give scholars the time and the freedom to contemplate the universe, to partake of the wisdom of the past, to add their small measure to the understanding of that wisdom, and to transmit the great tradition to certain chosen member of the younger generation."[43]

As universities grew into fragmented 'multiversities,' Grant saw the declining potential of philosophy departments to help students see how their particular fields of study relate to the whole of culture (justice societies) and the whole of the universe (in relation to God / the Good).[44] "[Philosophy's] purpose is to relate and see in unity all techniques, so that the physicist for instance can relate his activity to the fact of moral freedom, the economist see the productive capacity of his nation in relation to the Love of God."[45] But fulfilling this mandate is impossible apart from considering philosophy's dependence upon faith, a requirement that was largely off the grid of Anderson and his entourage. Grant laments,

> Philosophers in Western society have joined in the aspirations of the scientific age. The lie that knowledge exists only to provide power has been as much in the soul of philosophers as in the rest of society … pragmatism and positivism….
>
> Associated with the philosopher's willingness to make his subject serve the interests of physical science has been the dream of modern philosophy—that it might free itself from its traditional dependence upon the theological dogmas of faith.[46]

Grant resists reason unguided in faith by recounting the global tragedies[47] birthed through the marriage of faith-free liberal willing and amoral technologies:

> Unless philosophy is to become a purely negative discipline, it must have some kind of dependence on faith—whatever faith that may be. Reason not guided by faith cannot but find itself in the position of destroying everything and establishing nothing.[48]

Not that people of faith are absolved. Unreasoned faith is just as dangerous as faithless rationalism. "Society will suffer the tragedy of men looking for their faiths outside the rational discipline that it is the function of philosophy to provide in the search for faith."[49] Overall, Grant's assertion is that a healthy philosophy *is* a rational contemplation of the whole of reality in relation to the Good/God. Only philosophy so taught can lead society into "a contemplative tradition strong enough to act as a brake on the rightly impetuous men of action."[50]

In case Grant had not already discredited himself with the establishment philosophers, he sharpens his point for a final lunge:

> In closing, the present writer has no alternative but to repeat once again his conviction that the practice of philosophy (and for that matter, the arts of all civilization) will depend on a prior condition—namely the intensity and concentration of our faith in God. ... without such faith it will be vain to expect any great flowering of our culture in general and of our philosophy in particular.[51]

Grant would never be so publicly frank again about his faith, but the damage was done. Anderson flew into a tirade of denunciations among his colleagues across the campus and throughout his Canadian philosophical network. He spared no energy in reacting, convening a conference and publication at the University of Toronto entitled, *Philosophy in Canada: A Symposium*.[52] Much ado to make the point that Grant's essay should be regarded as insignificant! Anderson's introduction to the written work comprises one barrage after another, thereby pronouncing the establishment's verdict: anathema.

George was able to retreat to Nova Scotia to lick his wounds and ponder more indirect forays into the academy's minefields.[53] His counterattacks after this were more oblique but much more severe. For example, he admitted privately that his pejorative article, "Pursuit of an Illusion: A Commentary on Bertrand Russell," was written as a complete confutation of Anderson *et al* and a reiteration of his faith, though written indirectly.[54] He would "answer them in the long years of writing philosophy."[55]

### 3. 1950–59: Philosophy in the Mass Age

Throughout the 1950's, Grant kept his nose to the grindstone at Dalhousie: reading, teaching, writing, CBC radio talks, and most of all, thinking—rather, most of all, having babies with Sheila (six by the end of the decade). During those years he had the time to see cracks in previous monoliths like Augustine, Kant, Hegel, Marx, and Dewey. He also discovered and began to meditate upon new voices, guides along the path who could provide direction. We will discuss them momentarily, but for now, suffice it to say that Grant's grand discovery of the posthumous writings of Simone Weil came in 1950.[56] Simone Weil (1909–43) was a French secular Jew, philosophy teacher and essayist, political and labour activist, Christian Platonist, and afflicted mystic.[57] Grant believed she was a genuine modern saint, 'a flame'[58] whose life and thought confirmed and deepened his own experience, conversion, and doctrines (as we shall see in detail throughout this study). Eventually, he came to regard her has his highest authority next to the Gospels.[59]

Based on Grant's writings, Frank Flinn refers to this period (1945–1959) as "The Time of Chastened Hope," which culminates in the publication of *Philosophy in the Mass Age* (1959, reprinted 1966).[60] In this stage, Grant is still clinging to the *hope* of some sort of Hegelian synthesis between antiquity (time as "the moving image of an unmoving eternity"[61]) and modernity (time as man's unfolding history). He was also calling for:

> A new kind of transcendence which could encompass a vision of nature which is to be contemplated and a vision of nature which is to be dominated. At this time Grant was only dimly aware that he had posed a contradiction which did not lend itself to a mediation in the Hegelian mold.[62]

Even after the war, he still "came to believe that [Hegel's] idea of progress working itself out in the world was something one could believe and hold"—the work of providence whether or not one believed in Christianity.[63] The chastening comes as Grant's perception of the liberal vision of human nature = human freedom = history-making = progress was, in practice, unraveling on every front (whether in Marxism or western pragmatism). If social justice is our measure of the integrity of a philosophy,

Hegel's proffered hopes—the forward march of liberty, unfolding in history—were not panning out.

The 1950s became the essential decade for Grant in clarifying his understanding of Hegel versus Plato in the context of his discussions and debates with James Doull.[64] For Grant, Hegel treated the Greek classical era as an older, less-developed way of understanding that had been superceded by the progressivist unfolding of truth in the dialectic of history. But to Grant, Plato was the summation of all truth from which we have been progressively deteriorating. Grant and Doull finally broke over these two great philosophical traditions, a break exacerbated by personal tensions, perhaps due in part to Doull's jealousy of Grant's rising national public profile.

By *Philosophy in the Mass Age*, Grant's transition book, he sees the problem of Hegelian progressive modernism clearly. He counters with the language of natural law and promotes a mytho-poetic way of knowing. He pits the mythical-mystical-ethical way of knowing in the classical tradition against modernity as a way to demonstrate its unfolding. Grant holds high the classical and ancient vision (not just Plato, but especially Plato) that says there is an order in the universe to which we must attune ourselves.

### 4. 1960: The York Clash (or Fulton's Revenge)

In 1960, Grant moved to Toronto to work at the newly formed York University. He was promised, as founding chairman of the department, the freedom to build the kind of philosophy department that he felt was needed.[65] Only after he took the position did he find out that York was initially under temporary jurisdiction of the University of Toronto[66] (hereafter U of T) and therefore under the vindictive thumb of Fulton H. Anderson! Anderson informed Grant that he was to teach an introductory philosophy course *identical* to that at U of T and that the student's must write the U of T final exams and be marked by

U of T examiners. Further, he assigned Grant the primary textbook for the course, *The Spirit of Philosophy* by Marcus Long (a book that "made fun of Christianity and of Platonism"[67]). Long (secretary to the department) then presumed to dictate to Grant the outline of what must and must not be included in the first year course. It was too much. Grant, the first appointed academic at York University, was also the first to resign.[68]

### 5. 1961: McMaster and the Interfaith Connection

After some time casting about for work, Grant was invited to McMaster University as a faculty member in their expanding religious studies department. He saw this as his opportunity to teach Christian doctrine to non-divinity students in a Canadian university.[69] He could now relax about drawing a fine line between philosophy and Christianity as was expected at Dalhousie. From 1961 to 1980, McMaster would be a base from which Grant could freely explore the intellectual union of Greek philosophy and biblical religion—his synthesis of Athens (Socrates) and Jerusalem (Christianity)—and their relevance to the issue of justice in modern society and Canadian politics.

McMaster would also become a strong interfaith venue where Grant could expand his contemplative and peacemaking horizons, especially concerning Indian thought. His grandfather, George Munro Grant, had written one of Canada's first interfaith texts, *The Religions of the World* (1895).[70] And after meditating on Weil's *Notebooks*, Grant was well aware of the affinities between the Vedanta, Platonism, and Eastern forms of Christianity. At McMaster, the Department of Religious Studies of the 1960's–70's would develop "one of the best undergraduate and graduate programmes in North America in Indian thought."[71] Grant played a role in hiring some of McMaster's distinguished Indian studies scholars: John Arapura, Paul Younger, Khrishna Sivaraman, Bithika Mukerji, and Harold Coward.[72]

McMaster afforded Grant a rich venue for dialogue where

he could thread together Christ's Sermon on the Mount / Beatitudes with Ghandi's Satyagraha/Ahimsa in their respective calls to contemplative peacemaking.[73] In his 1966 "A Critique of the New Left,"[74] Grant cites Ghandi's example to appeal for our freedom and social activism to be rooted in truth-content and a contemplative knowledge of reality. Note Grant's prime doctrines throughout:

> The central Christian platitude still holds good. 'The truth shall make you free.' I use freedom here quite differently from those who believe that we are free when we have gained mastery over man and over nature. It is different even from the simple cry for political liberty: 'Freedom now.' For in the long pull freedom without the knowledge of reality is empty and vacuous. The greatest figure of our era, Gandhi, was interested in public actions and in political liberty, but he knew that the right direction of that action had to be based on knowledge of reality—with all the discipline and order and study that that entailed.[75]

Like Weil, "Grant saw himself as standing within the 'Hindu wing of Christianity', … he thought the contemplative and mystical core of Christianity made it 'closer to Hinduism' that to either the Jewish or Islamic traditions."[76] Like Thomas Merton in the United States, Grant was, "as a Canadian, at the forefront of probing greater contemplative depths in the Christian tradition; and by doing so, open[ed] up new trails for interfaith dialogue."[77]

### 6. 1965: University of Toronto 'Teach-in' and *Lament*

Two events signal 1965 as George Grant's ascent to preeminence as Canada's national philosopher: the release of his most influential book, *Lament for a Nation*, and his part in the International Teach-in at the University of Toronto (Oct. 1965).

*Lament for a Nation: the Defeat of Canadian Nationalism* has been hailed as a "passionate defense of our Canadian identity ... of enduring importance ... [to] be respected as a masterpiece of political meditation."[78] The book was a best-seller in Canada, propelling Grant to national prominence. Politician James Laxer writes, "*Lament for a Nation* is the most important book I have ever read in my life. Here was a crazy old philosopher of religion at McMaster and he woke up half our generation. He was saying Canada is dead, and by saying it he was creating the country."[79] Journalist David Cayley testifies, "*Lament for a Nation* had a curious, even paradoxical effect. You presented it as a lament, but among younger people like me, it helped to galvanize a new nationalism."[80]

Others could not see it. For example, Robin Mathews, "Crown Prince of Canadian Political Poets," wrote a poetic response to *Lament* entitled "The Wave of the Future."[81] He assaults *Lament's* theorizing from the perspective of the activists, accusing Grant of abandoning them in the political trenches. Grant replied,

> Thank you for your letter and poem. The poem is indeed insulting, as it accuses me of lack of courage, and what is worse, valetudinarianism. I do not think I lack hope, because in the Christian sense I interpret hope as a supernatural virtue, and courage is what is necessary in the world.[82]

Grant's diagnosis, bleak as it sounded, functioned with specific aims and did so effectively.

As a political statement indicting American interventionist foreign policy, *Lament* caught the interest of the anti-Vietnam War movement and Canada's 'New Left.' University students were holding campus 'teach-ins' combining sit-in protest and lectures across North America. When Charles Hanly (of U of T) presented the idea of an international teach-in during a University of Michigan meeting, Toronto was proposed as a neutral(ish) venue where they could focus on the theme of 'Revolution.' Grant was invited because of his "new left, conservative, nationalist, anti-American views."[83] He spoke to a large crowd on 'Protest and Technology,' denouncing those that "believe that by some dialectical process of history there should suddenly spring out of this technological system a free and humane society."[84] By now a master of formulating questions, Grant concludes with this sequel to *Lament*:

> We must not delude ourselves and we must not throw up our hands. Where in this mammoth system can we use our intelligence and our love to open up areas where human excellence can exist? How can we use the most effective pressure to see that the empire of which we are a satellite uses moderation and restraint in its relations with the rest of the world? ... Our greatest obligation as Canadian citizens is to work for a country which is not simply a satellite of any empire.[85]

Grant's nephew, Michael Ignatieff, was involved in the sit-in and present for the speech. Recalling Grant's lament in both the book and the speech, he recalls,

> The Canadians who heard him that day believed he was actually calling for a revival of Canadian nationalism, and they took him at his word. He may have counseled fatalism [?] but, happily, Canadians did not listen. Ironically, he played his part in reviving a political debate about Canada and its relation to the United States that endures to this day.[86]

Grant's previous considerable political interest and activity now found a popular national stage. He would use that stage over the coming decades as a noted political scientist and philosopher. Sometimes his courage and notoriety in that role obscures the animating core that generated the *what* and the *why* of his vocation: he was a contemplative theologian and thus, more than a political philosopher and activist. He engaged the arena of justice and peace as a prophet in the traditions of Jeremiah and Jesus, whose Beatitudes comprised the central core to Grant's ethical vision.[87]

### Endnotes

1. I have recounted and analyzed Grant's conversion in detail in my thesis, *We Are Not Our Own: The Platonic Christianity of George Grant* (2012).

2. Grant, "Canada: An Introduction to a Nation," *CW* 1: 74–90; Grant, "The Empire: Yes or No?" *CW* 1: 97–126.

3. William Christian, "Behind Every Great Man …," *History Wire* (2009). Christian estimates that Sheila wrote at least five of the essays that bear George Grant's name.

4. Cayley, *GC*, 56.

5. Larry Schmidt, *GP*, 64.

6. Wayne Hankey, "James Doull, Étienne Gilson and George Grant on Modernity and Platonism," *The Friend* 2.1 (2000): 18–21.

7. GPG to David Dodds, 11/11/1986. "It was the first Socratic meeting of the year so C.S.L. was speaking. What sense! What clarity! What importance! It was just what I had come back to Oxford to hear. My breath was taken away with gladness. From then on the Socratic Club was a centre for me." (William Christian, *SL*, 361).

8. William Christian, *Biography* (1994), 115.

9. E.g., Austin Farrer, *Love Almighty and Ills Unlimited* (1961); C. S. C. S. Lewis, *The Problem of Pain* (1941). Cf. Oswald Bayer, *Living by Faith* (2003), 11.

10. Cayley, *GC*, 52–3. "He taught me how to read [philosophy]." Cf. GPG to Dearest Ould, 05/30/1946 (Jersak, *MSO* 14.9). GPG to Dearest Ould, 11/14/1946 (Christian, *SL*, 137–9).

11. Of Farrer, Grant said, "I had the only direct vision I ever had. I saw

the golden eagle of St John descend upon him." (Schmidt, *GP*, 63).

12. Christian, *Biography* (1994), 149.

13. Cayley, *GC*, 52.

14. GPG to Mumps, 06/17/1940 (Jersak, *MSO* 14.10).

15. GPG to Derek Bedson (Bedson Private Papers, Prov. of Manitoba Archives), received 07/02/1964. (Christian, *Biography* (1994), 245). Cf. Larry Schmidt and George Grant, "An Interview with George Grant (*Grail*)," *CW* 4: 566–7.

16. Grant, "The Theology of John Oman," *CW* 1: 157–419.

17. GPG to Mother, 11/03/1945 (Christian, *SL*, 122).

18. Forbes, *Guide to His Thought*, 172; Grant, "The Theology of John Oman," *CW* 1: 222.

19. Grant, "The Theology of John Oman," *CW* 1: 161–2, 170, 188.

20. Grant, "The Theology of John Oman," *CW* 1: 170, 213, 220.

21. Grant, "The Theology of John Oman," *CW* 1: 171, 175, 220, 299, 301, 367.

22. Grant, "The Theology of John Oman," *CW* 1: 171, 188, 345. On the Calvinist-Puritan roots of liberal political triumphalism, see Grant, "The Theology of John Oman," *CW* 1: 346; Grant, *Technology and Empire* (1969), 21, 37.

23. Grant, "The Theology of John Oman," *CW* 1: 267.

24. Grant, "Two Theological Languages," *Two Theological Languages* (1990), 6–19.

25. Grant, "Review of *The Philosophy of Francis Bacon*," *CW* 1: 147–8.

26. Grant, "Review of *The Philosophy of Francis Bacon*," *CW* 1: 147; Christian, *Biography* (1994), 152–3.

27. Christian, *Biography* (1994), 151.

28. John G. Slater, *Minerva's Aviary* (2005), 338–41. Grant's attack on Bacon and his interpretation of Plato would have been especial sore

points for Anderson, whose books on those philosophers headlined his expertise.

29. E.g., C. S. Lewis, *The Discarded Image: An Introduction to Medieval and Renaissance Literature* (1964).

30. Gilson founded the Pontifical Institute of Medieval Studies at St. Michaels (U of T) in 1929.

31. Cf. Leslie Armour and Elizabeth Trott, *The Faces of Reason: Philosophy in English Canada, 1850–1950* (1981).

32. Grant, "Philosophy – The Massey Commission Report," *CW* 2: 9–11.

33. William Christian, "George Grant and Religion," *Journal of Canadian Studies* (1991): 43.

34. Grant, "Philosophy," *CW* 2: 3.

35. Grant, "Philosophy," *CW* 2: 7–8, 11.

36. Grant, "Philosophy," *CW* 2: 4.

37. Grant, "Philosophy," *CW* 2: 4.

38. Grant, "Philosophy," *CW* 2: 11.

39. Grant, "Philosophy," *CW* 2: 6, 12.

40. Grant, "Philosophy," *CW* 2: 13.

41. Grant, "Philosophy," *CW* 2: 19.

42. Grant, "Philosophy," *CW* 2: 4.

43. Grant, "Philosophy," *CW* 2: 4.

44. Grant, "Philosophy," *CW* 2: 10, 13, 17–20.

45. Grant, "Philosophy," *CW* 2: 6.

46. Grant, "Philosophy," *CW* 2: 7–8.

47. "It is out of a sense of tragedy and uncertainty more than anything else that the need for philosophical speculation arises." (Grant, "Philosophy," *CW* 2: 6; cf. 8, 12).

48. Grant, "Philosophy," *CW* 2: 8, 10, 12.

49. Grant, "Philosophy," *CW* 2: 8.

50. Grant, "Philosophy," *CW* 1: 19.

51. Grant, "Philosophy," *CW* 1: 20.

52. GPG to Maude Grant, 1952 (Jersak, *MSO* 14.11). Grant, "Philosophy," *CW* 2: 3; F. H. Anderson, "Introduction," *Philosophy in Canada* (1952), 2, 4; Slater, *Minerva's Aviary* (2005), 339.

53. GPG to Dearest Ould, 1952 (Christian, *SL*, 174–6).

54. GPG to Dearest Ould, 09/13/1952 (Jersak, *MSO* 14.12).

55. GPG to Dearest Ould, 1952 (Jersak, *MSO* 14.13).

56. Heaven, "Some Influences of Simone Weil," *GP*, 68. Grant first gave a review of Weil's *Waiting on God* on CBC Radio, 12/16/1952. Grant, "Appendix 3: Radio and Television Broadcasts," *CW* 2: 536.

57. Grant, "Adult Education in the Expanding Economy," *CW* 2: 109.

58. Heaven, "Some Influences of Simone Weil," 74.

59. Grant, "Simone Weil," *GGR*, 237.

60. Frank Flinn, "Bibliographical Introduction," *GP*, 195.

61. Cf. Plato, *Timaeus* 37d.

62. Flinn, "Bibliographical Introduction," *GP*, 196–7.

63. Cayley, *GC*, 65.

64. James Doull was Grant's friend and colleague at Dalhousie, a leading Canadian Hegelian and apologist of liberalism. The emphasis then was on individuality, choice, and consciousness. Cf. Hankey, "Modernity and Platonism," *The Friend* 2.1 (2000): 18–21.

65. Interview with Paul Axelrod, 02/16/1977 (Christian, *Biography* (1994), 199).

66. GPG to Murray Ross, 02/27/1960 (Christian, *SL*, 199–200). Cayley, *GC*, 92–3.

67. Cayley, *GC*, 93.

68. GPG to Murray Ross, 04/14/1960 (Christian, *SL*, 201–2). Slater,

*Minerva's Aviary* (2005), 340–1.

69. Christian, *Biography* (1994), 209–10.

70. His Christian triumphalism notwithstanding. Cf. Mendelson, *Exiles from Nowhere* (2008).

71. Dart, *Spiders and Bees* (2008), 156.

72. R. S. Dart, "Michael Ignatieff, Grant, and India," *CICS Report* 4.3 (2009): 6.

73. Grant, "Five Lectures on Christianity," *Athens and Jerusalem* (2006), 229; Dart, *Spiders and Bees* (2008), 159–60, 171.

74. Grant, "A Critique of the New Left," *GGR*, 84–90.

75. Grant, "A Critique of the New Left," *GGR*, 89.

76. Dart, *Spiders and Bees* (2008), 167; Cayley, *GC*, 176; Schmidt, *GP*, 102. Cf. Grant, "Introduction" to Bithika Mukerji [Grant's student], *Neo-Vedanta and Modernity* (1983); John G. Arapura [Grant's colleague], "Modern Thought and the Transcendent," *Modernity and Responsibility* (1983); Sheila Grant, "George Grant and the Theology of the Cross," *George Grant and the Subversion of Modernity* (1996); and Arati Barua, *Ghandi and Grant* (2010).

77. Dart, *Spiders and Bees* (2008), 167.

78. Peter C. Emberley, "Foreword to the Carleton Library Edition," *Lament*, lxxvii–lxxviii.

79. Charles Taylor, *Radical Tories* (1982), 148.

80. Cayley, *GC*, 107.

81. Robin Mathews, "Wave of the Future," *This Time, This Place* (1965). Ron Dart, *Robin Mathews: Crown Prince of Canadian Political Poets* (2002), 34.

82. GPG to Robin Mathews, 07/14/1965 (Christian, *SL*, 229).

83. Charles Hanly to Ron Dart, personal correspondence, 06/21/2009; Charles Hanly (ed.), *Revolution and Response: Selections from the Toronto International Teach-in* (1966), vii–xvii.

84. Grant, "Protest and Technology," *Revolution and Response* (1996), 124.

85. Grant, "Protest and Technology," *Revolution and Response* (1996), 128.

86. Michael Ignatieff, *True Patriot Love* (2009), 147. Note Ignatieff's failure to perceive Grant's self-aware employment of lament as a powerful rhetorical device. Lament is purposely ironic by definition, for when it works, what sounds like a dirge actually triggers an awakening.

87. Dart, *Spiders and Bees* (2008), 171.

# Part 3

# Divine Consent

# 7

# Wrath and Love as Divine Consent

> God does no violence to secondary causes in the accomplishment of his ends.
> —Simone Weil[1]

I close this work with a lateral move to creatively apply Grant's divine consent towards a metaphorical reading of *wrath* back into those Scriptures that so repulsed him and Weil. If God operates in the world by consent, they might have seen wrath, not as the retribution of a wilful God, but as a metaphor (as they saw *power*) for the consequences of God's consent to our non-consent. After appropriating Grantean consent to 'demetaphorise' wrath, I will scrutinize a potential pitfall in Weil that Grant avoided in practicing consent: the pressure to consent well enough in order to manipulate outcomes, which subtly sabotages true consent.

In this section, I intend to apply this cosmology of consent to the problem of how we read 'wrath' in the Hebrew and Christian Scriptures. The texts where God intervenes with smoldering vengeance were an offense to Grant and Weil as they portray a God of personal wrath through violent force—the willful *uber-Gott* (my term) they rejected. Grant and Weil warn us not to literalize metaphors or personalize anthropomorphisms, only to dismiss many of those passages for speaking metaphorically. Why not apply their theology of the Cross and cosmology of consent as a hermeneutical lens for demetaphorising the Bible's judgment narratives, and so retrieving them?[2]

The following is a Grantean attempt to do so, specifically as I would address it sermonically to Evangelicals,[3] who tend to be most entangled in literalism, though it might also be beneficial to skeptics who, like Grant and Weil, find the Bible repulsive because they too read it overly literally. I will also apply Grantean consent to model how one might preach a love above and beyond wrath, where "mercy triumphs over judgement" (James 2:13).

### Sermonic application

God is good.
God is love.
God is not violent, because he never does violence directly.

In His love, God will not bring about his ends through directly violent means.

But in refusing to exercise such violence, God consents to our violence.

His love consents to our violence against each other. And against God.

God's consent is not complicity.

But God appears complicit in our violence because God allows it.

That is, when God refuses to apply force, might, and violence but instead, consents to our free rebellion and its bitter and violent fruit, God seems violent in His consent.

In love, God consents to our wrath on the Cross.
He consents to our wrath against 'Rome.'
He consents to Rome's wrath against us.

His consent is wrath.
His consent is love.[4]

And so, in the Bible, where we see or hear of God's *wrath*, we are usually, actually seeing God's nonviolent consent to the natural and supernatural forces of the world and of human freedom. God's wrath is consent to allowing, and not sparing, the powerful consequences of these forces to take their course. We say natural *and supernatural*, because (a) God's order of secondary causes extends beyond our empirical or rational categories, and (b) the natural and supernatural interrelate beyond observation or comprehension. And they mysteriously inter-relate with our own power of consent to 'bind and loose' (Matt. 16:19) through love and prayer, to intercede in ways that might spare someone the consequences of these 'laws.'

What of God's wrath? Did God not slaughter Egypt's firstborn (Exod. 12)? Did God not massacre the Jewish grumblers in the wilderness (Num. 26)? Did God not incinerate Sodom and Gomorrah (Gen. 19) or repeatedly reduce Jerusalem to smoking rubble (Jer. 52)? Did God not strike down Ananias and Sapphira at Peter's feet (Acts 5) or eat Herod alive with worms (Acts 12:23)?

No.

And Yes.

First, no. Were these acts of violent intervention by an angry and punitive God who was reacting to sin? No. The causes of death are ascribed to 'the Destroyer,' to angelic or human agents of violence, or to Satan (Exod. 12:23; Gen. 19:13; Jer. 4:7; 1 Cor. 10:9–10; Acts 5:3). God protects or ceases to harbour potential victims, depending on someone's *consent* (or not) through repentance, surrender, or intercession (cf. Abraham in Gen. 18, or Moses in Exod. 33).

Second, yes. These were acts of *God's wrath* in that God consented to allow natural and supernatural destruction to take its course through events set in motion by human decisions. In that sense, we read that God is seen to have 'sent' the destroyer and 'sent' the destruction—God is perceived as commissioning the destruction or even as the destroyer (Exod. 12:29; Gen. 19:14; Num. 21:6).

But in Romans 1 (possibly picking up from Isa. 64:5–7), Paul clarifies: what had been described in the narrative metaphorically as a seemingly active wrath is in fact the 'giving over' (God's consent) of rebellious people to their own self-destructive trajectories—even when the shrapnel of our actions accrues collateral damage on innocents! When in Romans 5 we read that God in Christ was saving us from 'the wrath,' we are not to believe that Jesus is saving us from God, but from the consequences of sin (death, according to Rom. 6:23) imbedded in the very order of the universe.

Still, what of those who challenge God: "How can you allow this? Is your permission—your giving over—not tantamount to complicity?"

And the answer is probably yes—if not complicity, ultimate responsibility as first cause—such that some biblical authors use the phrase 'wrath of God' to describe what are technically secondary consequences. Ultimately, this is God's good order and God is finally responsible for all that is.

This is the great and terrible price of choosing to save the world through love. Saving the world through love means allowing horrible things that make God look both wrathful and weak all at once.

God's nonviolent consent extends to the whole of natural and spiritual reality. It includes nonviolent consent to human freedom, for good or ill. It includes nonviolent consent to the laws of nature, for beauty or tragedy, creation or destruction. It includes nonviolent consent to spiritual laws of sowing and reaping, blessing and cursing. In this sense, God's consent means that God has renounced the exercise of his Almighty capacities in this world.

The Lamb already slain before the foundation of the world died to being all-powerful before Creation. This kenotic self-renunciation has made space for creation. For freedom and for violence. For genocide and hurricanes and car accidents and pedophiles.

But also for love.

God's nonviolent consent and self-emptying space makes room for God's love in the universe and in humankind.

God has sown supernatural love into the very fabric of the world; a love that not only consents to violence but also subverts and overcomes violence. Far from feeble in this nonviolent consent, God's love is powerful—the only conceivable power—that can make all things right and new. God's love does not need to violate the freedom or the laws of that which exists through interventions that suspend natural and spiritual order, because *love is the ground* of all that exists. Love is part of that order—its essential heart. At the top of that order is humanity, with the created capacity to be like God, that is, to consent to bear and seed God's supernatural love throughout all of creation.

Somehow, though, we know—we see with our own eyes and hear with our own ears—something is broken, has ruptured. All of creation and, most of all, humanity groans under an affliction whereby God's consent to violence seems to enslave us rather than free us. Or perhaps that God's loving consent to our freedom has born the fruit of violence rather than love. Our very freedom has become the violent means of our slavery.

From that point of view, God seems cruel, whether through absence or complicity. God seems impotent, for how can God possibly mend a breach that God's love and our freedom ultimately created?

Thanks be to God, at the pinnacle of humanity stands Jesus Christ. His nonviolent consent to the Cross—the intersection of humanity's affliction (our freedom-to-violence) and God's radical forgiveness—becomes the occasion whereby supernatural love flows through God's own wounds into the world. That love, far from being weak or impotent, will eclipse violence, might, and force as the relentless catalyst for the renewal of the world.

The Lordship of Christ (or the Kingdom of God) over the world and the universe is not contradictory to God's nonviolent consent. In fact, consent is precisely (and only) how God's love is released in the world. One example: in the Gospels, Christ did not operate in the power of miraculous interventions (the magical suspension of laws), but in the authority of supernatural love (the application of God's highest law).

We have suggested that God's Kingdom does not advance through violence, freedom-violating force, or law-breaking interventions. God's kingdom reign is the advance of supernatural love in and through those who consent to being indwelt and transformed by Christ-mediated love. Here we are not just talking about enthusiastic activists performing good and loving works. But neither is this consent restricted to Christian churchgoers. Rather, this consent is defined in 1 John 4:7–8: "Dear friends, let us love one another, for love comes from God. *Everyone who loves has been born of God and knows God.* Whoever does not love does not know God, *because God is love*."

Through their own nonviolent consent, such lovers may appear as torn veils or cracked vessels (2 Cor. 4:7–18), but through their wounds, supernatural love pours its healing light into natural realm, permeating the world.

God consents to our reluctance to consent, resulting in this painfully slow but inexorable transfiguration of our violent world.

Love *will* have its way, because while it may look like passive consent to extreme violence, it is nevertheless "stronger than death, more jealous than the grave, more vehement than a flame. Many waters cannot quench love, nor floods drown it"

(Song of Songs 8:6–7). The death and resurrection of Christ are the firstfruits of the destiny God's love has arranged for the whole universe.

**Sermonic explanation**

By way of explanation, Grant and Weil are right in seeing many hegemonic descriptions of the Kingdom of God in the Hebrew Scriptures (i.e., examples of the violent and willful God of wrath). Instead of dismissing them immediately, as Weil often does, a Grantean hermeneutic invites investigation into three broad possibilities. I will illustrate these with the phrase, "God, the king who is angry" and comment on each approach.

a. *God may literally be an angry King.* God actively decreed that Israel should go to war, obliterate, and enslave their enemies, or suffer God's wrath through those enemies. In this view, Jesus comes to introduce a New Covenant, altering how God deals with people in the New Kingdom. This typically Evangelical interpretation falls short of Grant's God who was, is, and always will be the perfection of goodness and love. Such texts are sufficiently toxic to be discarded *or* valuable and inspired warnings of how God's people continue to worship their own shadows and baptize their own violence.

b. *God may not be an angry King at all.* The Old Testament characters and authors infer emotions, reactions, and destruction through hegemonic filters that misrepresent the nature of God as love. In this view Jesus comes to reveal the true nature of the Kingdom of God as shalomic. In truth, God has never been hegemonic but has been reduced to an idol through our anthropomorphisms, even in our Scriptures. This comes closest to Grant and Weil's view, and they have little patience for extracting divine truth from errant human projections. Jesus, on the other hand, made use of such texts by way of contrast, "You have heard that it has been said … But I say to you" (Matt. 5:21, 38) to demonstrate the superior authority of his teaching.

c. *God may be a metaphorically angry King.* In the above sermon, I take up Grant and Weil's suggestion (but not their example) concerning the wrath texts, conceding that God's so-called anger is a metaphor, whereas God's loving rule includes *consenting* to our self-destructive ways and their consequences. God is not actually angry, but we experience God's wrath as God's passive and indirect consent to destructive forces of necessity. The wrath texts thus serve as valuable warnings of real destruction but ought not be literalized into direct threats from a hateful God. In this view, Jesus also freely but advisedly uses the metaphor of an angry King in some of his parables—a concession to our phenomenology of wrath—but through the New Covenant, trumps that metaphor with a better one—Father of unconditional love—to which the sermon finally points.

My broader point is that an informing theology of consent makes sense of both God's wrath and love without the pitfalls of providential intervention, even where they are described that way in the Bible. But a pitfall does circle a practical theology of consent.

### Potential pitfall: Consent as coercion

A spirituality of consent may preach well, but it presents a difficulty if we believe God only operates in the world through human participation. While I subscribe to this tenet of Grant's faith, it can become an oppressive burden if we follow Weil too mechanically. Specifically, if I believe God's response is directly proportional to the fervency of my desire and attention, the final outcome seems to rest on me. I need only consent sufficiently and God *must* answer. Weil said as much:

> For the desire, oriented toward God, is the only force capable of raising the soul. Or rather, it is God alone who comes to possess and lift the soul, but only desire obliges God to descend. He only comes to those who ask him to come; and those who ask him often, for a long time,

and ardently. He cannot prevent himself from coming to them.[5]

We might call this the pitfall of consent-as-coercion *if* we slip back into willful mastery of world conditions, this time by managing God's saving participation through coercive contemplation. We might suppose that God *expects* us to manage the world and even to save it by finally discovering the right recipe of consent that releases God to act. Such pressure, if taken seriously, would crush us. In Grant's humility, he did not trip on this delusion. His McMaster sermon explicitly confesses our frailty in consent and opts instead to contemplate the perfection of Christ's consent. Grant identifies with Luther's despair of self and casts himself on the sufficiency of the Cross.

By contrast, part of Weil thrived on such pressure, willed such crushing—and in the end, by coveting it, perchance succumbed to it. In part, Weil died because she was forbidden from sacrificing herself to save France. When her redemptive consent to parachute back into France—and probable martyrdom—was rejected by Charles de Gaul, it crushed her.

By analogy, a similar pressure accompanies certain types of faith healing movements when they say:
- It is always God's will to heal.
- If you ask in faith ('name it, claim it'), God will heal.
- If you are not healed, it is because you (or we) don't have enough faith.

I do not believe we can live that way, except in denial. We would be right to feel such a burden as impossible—or rise (fall) into a Messiah complex.

Thankfully, Weil's theology of consent is more textured than that. First, God consents for the world to exist as it does, including evils experienced through the gravity of natural law and the wilfulness of semi-free people. Somehow, consenting to such a universe (without endorsing the particulars) is also God's will.

Second, I too must consent for the world to exist as it does, including the evils experienced through the gravity of natural law and the wilfulness of semi-free people. The Stoics, Nietzsche, and Weil all call this *amor fati*. The recovery community calls it *acceptance*. Theologians of the Cross say, '*It is what it is.*' Accepting God's consent for the world to exist as it does negates Pentecostal triumphalism, providential micro-management, and its secular counterpart in progressivist optimism.

*But*, third, I can consent to and welcome the seeds of God's grace into the world through my life via surrender. And because I have an idea of what those seeds might be (supernatural love), I might also have clues about the fruit they might produce. The trick is that consent requires openness and surrender, quite the opposite to my habitual striving and intercessory manipulation. In the paragraph following the one that concerned me above, Weil says,

> Attention is an effort, perhaps the greatest of all efforts, but it is a negative effort. By itself, it does not involve fatigue. When fatigue is felt, attention is nearly impossible, unless one has already had good practice; one is then better to abandon it, to search for some peace, then a little later to recommence, detaching oneself and resuming as one inhales and exhales.[6]

Contemplatives like Grant or Weil become sensitive to the overtures of divine love, but remain detached from trying to forcibly wring fruit from the Vine. Rather, by consent and attention—*abiding* in the Vine (John 15)—they receive God's life and allow fruit-bearing to happen in its time as it will.

Revivalist triumphalism, by contrast, misses all three of these points to various degrees. But in my view Weil's system is still open to critique.

She presents this process as analogous to an invariable mechanism. If one surrenders fully, decreates one's ego sufficiently, pays attention perfectly, and loves unswervingly, then God's answer will be invariable and automatic. Imagine: the electricity is always on and available—we need only be plugged-in, functional, switched-on spiritual appliances. Apart from electricity, a toaster can do nothing. But apart from a toaster, electricity won't toast bread. Weil is so confident in God's answer according to our faith[7] she makes the universal fixed order of God sound like a beneficent vending machine. And maybe it is. Christ himself describes faith as if it were as reliable as gravity. *But* here are my objections:

First, Weil does not entirely resolve the problem of Pentecostal triumphalism powered by sufficient faith. She has only displaced it with a contemplative mechanism powered by sufficient surrender and attention. The temptation is still there to succumb to pressurized striving—'trying to surrender enough'—in order to produce the results we believe God wants. Producing results as our agenda, ironically, seems a sure sign that we haven't surrendered the results. Here, those who subscribe to the power of attention in Weil must remain equally committed to her practice of acceptance.

Second, Weil does not deal with the persisting existential randomness of life, even if God is no longer seen as personally arbitrary. In our experience, sometimes we have truly surrendered and nevertheless get crucified; other times, with virtually no surrender or attention, mighty deeds occur in spite of us. The direct and predictable correlation that Weil implies between higher degrees of attention and observable results does not appear true in practice. Randomness persists, regardless of one's contemplative acumen.

She might counter with the obvious truth that in fact, the world of humanity, including the church, has not surrendered, or hardly at all. She might say that whatever pressure we feel or randomness we observe is entirely accounted for in our own wilfulness. She might quote D. L. Moody, who said, "The world has yet to see what God can do with and for and through and in and by the man who is fully and wholly consecrated to Him. I will try my utmost to be that man."[8]

To conclude this critique, I will side with Weil once again on two points. First, when she says that God only works in this world through human consent, this includes the ultimate ongoing mediation of the man, Jesus. For Weil, Gethsemane and Golgotha stand as twin events of perfect surrender through which grace floods the world. Transcendent goodness can pour through the torn veil of the fabric of the universe that we call Christ's body. A tear, by the way, which the NT regards as having never been sewn shut.

Second and finally, she also connects this torn veil with the torn veils of our own lives—not our perfections. This is exactly how I see the sacramentality of the tragic in a poet like Gerard Manley Hopkins[9] or a depressive like Logan Runnalls. In his critique of disability studies, Logan holds the Weilian tension as his own confession:

> What I understand (in my vague way) disability studies to be doing is erasing the tension we find in life. I'm not comfortable thinking of my depression as in the realms of good or unflawed. And yet I now believe that this is a really important way that I bear the image of Christ. I too am a "man of sorrows." I do not want to get rid of the tension between depression as flaw and depression as way of bearing the image of God. Nor do I see any reason to be compelled to. To do so is to give up on loving the Other and settling for a weak justice.[10]

Runnalls' tension is perfect commentary for Weil's *amor fati* and George Grant's theodicy of the Cross. His consent to God *and* to the reality of his depression becomes a means of grace in this world—or light in the cave.

## Endnotes

1. Weil, *IC*, 97.

2. Reading the Old Testament violence texts is once again a going concern. I am not aware of any applications of Weil's approach to these texts, even in Grant or Weil.

3. Hence the sermonic tone and format.

4. "Love is consent to authentic otherness." (Grant, *TJ*, 38).

5. Weil, *AD*, 71. My translation.

6. Weil, *AD*, 71–2. My translation.

7. And not without biblical warrant. Cf. John 14:12; 15:7; 1 John 5:14–15.

8. John Pollock, *Moody: The Biography* (1983), 115.

9. E.g., Girard Manley Hopkins, "The Wreck of the Deutschland," *Poems* (1919).

10. Logan Runnalls, 10/6/2011 (*Agora 2.0 newsgroup*).

# Abbreviations

## George Grant Books

ESJ  *English-Speaking Justice.* Sackville, NB: Mount Allison University, 1978. Toronto: Anansi Press and Notre Dame: Notre Dame Press, 1985. Toronto: Anansi Press, 1998.
Lament  *Lament for a Nation: the Defeat of Canadian Nationalism.* Toronto: McClelland & Stewart, 1965, 1970. Ottawa: Carleton University Press, 1994. Montreal / Kingston: McGill-Queen's University Press, 1995.
TE  *Technology and Empire: Perspectives on North America.* Toronto: House of Anansi Press, 1969.
TJ  *Technology and Justice.* Toronto: House of Anansi Press, 1986.
TH  *Time as History.* Toronto: University of Toronto Press, 1971, 1995.
PMA  *Philosophy in the Mass Age.* Toronto: Copp Clark, 1959. New York: Hill and Wang, 1959. Toronto: Copp Clark, 1966. Toronto: University of Toronto Press, 1995.

## George Grant Collections

CW 1  Davis, Arthur and Peter C. Emberley, eds. *Collected Works of George Grant: Volume 1* (1933–1950). Toronto: University of Toronto Press, 2000.
CW 2  Davis, Arthur, ed. *Collected Works of George Grant: Volume 2* (1951-1959). Toronto: University of Toronto Press, 2002.
CW 3  Davis, Arthur and Henry Roper, eds. *Collected Works of George Grant: Volume 3* (1960–1969). Toronto: University of Toronto Press, 2005.
CW 4  Davis Arthur and Henry Roper, eds. *Collected Works of George Grant: Volume 4* (1970?1988). Toronto: University of Toronto Press, 2009.
GGR  Christian, William and Sheila Grant, eds. *The George Grant Reader.* Toronto, Canada: University of Toronto Press, 1998.

*MSO* Jersak, Brad. *Minerva's Snowy Owl: Essays in Poltical Theology.* Abbotsford: Fresh Wind Press, 2012.

*SL* Christian, William, ed. *George Grant: Selected Letters* edited, with an introduction by William Christian. Toronto: University of Toronto Press, 1996.

**George Grant Interviews**

*GC* Cayley, David. *George Grant in Conversation.* Toronto: Anansi, 1995.
*GP* Schmidt, Larry, ed. *George Grant in Process.* Toronto: Anansi, 1978.

**Simone Weil (English)**

*FLN* *First and Last Notebooks*, Trans. Richard Rees. London / New York / Toronto: Oxford University Press, 1970.
*FW* *Formative Writings, 1929-1941.* Trans. D.T. McFarland and W Van Ness. Amherst: University of Massachusetts, 1987.
*G-G* *Gateway to God.* Ed. by David Raper. London: Fontana, 1974.
*G&G* *Gravity and Grace.* 1952. Trans. Emma Craufurd and Mario von dur Ruhr. London/New York: Routledge, 2002.
*IC* *Intimations of Christianity Among the Ancient Greeks.* 1957. Trans. Elisabeth Chas Geissbuhler. London/New York: Ark, 1987.
*LPh* *Lectures on Philosophy.* (Leçon de philosophie, Librairie Plon, 1959). Trans. Hugh Price. Cambridge: Cambridge University Press, 1978.
*LP* *Letter to a Priest.* 1954. Trans. A. F. Wills. New York: Penguin, 2003.
*NFR* *The Need for Roots: Prelude to a Declaration of Duties towards Mankind.* Trans. A. F. Wills. New York and London: Routledge, 1952.
*NB 1* *The Notebooks.* Trans. Arthur Wills. Volume 1. London: Routledge & Kegan Paul, 1956.
*NB 2* *The Notebooks.* Trans. Arthur Wills. Volume 2. London: Routledge & Kegan Paul, 1956.

*OL*    *Oppression and Liberty,* Amherst, MS: University of Massachusetts Press, 1973.
*SNL*   *On Science, Necessity, and the Love of God.* London, New York, Toronto: Oxford University Press, 1968.

*SWR*  *Simone Weil Reader.* Ed. George A. Panichas. Mt. Kisco, NY: Moyer Bell, Ltd., 1977.
*SE*    *Simone Weil: Selected Essays, 1934–43.* Trans. by Richard Rees. London: Oxford University Press, 1962.
*SL*    *Simone Weil: Seventy Letters.* Trans. by Richard Rees. London: Oxford University Press, 1965.
*SWW*  *Simone Weil: Writings Selected* with an Introduction by Eric O. Springsted. Modern Spiritual Masters Series. Maryknoll, NY: Orbis Books, 1998.
*TG*    *Thinking God: A Bilingual Simone Weil Reader.* Trans. Benjamin Bergery, 2002–05. <http://simoneweil.net/lesautres.htm>.
*WG*   *Waiting for God.* Trans. Emma Craufurd. New York: Harper, 1951, 2009.

**Simone Weil (French)**

*AD*   *Attente de Dieu* [Lettres écrites du 19 janvier au 26 mai 1942]. Éditions Fayard, 1966.
*CS*   *La Connaissance surnaturelle.* Paris: Gallimard, 1950.
*EHP*  *Écrits historiques et politiques.* Œuvres completes Tome II. Vol. 1. Éditions Gallimard, 1988.
*ELD*  *Écrits de Londres et dernières letters.* Paris: Gallimard, 1957.
*IPC*  *Intuitions pré-chrétiennes.* Nouvelle edition. Paris: Fayard, 1985.
*LR*   *Lettre à un religeiux.* Éditions Gallimard, 1951.
*Oeuvres*  *Oeuvres,* Quarto Gallimard, 1999.
*Pensées*  *Pensées sans ordre concernant l'amour de Dieu.* Paris: Gallimard, 1968.
*PG*  *La pesanteur et la grace.* Librairie Plon, 1947.
*SG*  *La Source grecque.* Paris: Gallimard, 1963.

# Bibliography

## George Grant: Primary Works

**Books and articles (chronologically) including editions**

1959    *Philosophy in the Mass Age.* Toronto: Copp Clark, 1959. New York: Hill and Wang, 1959. Toronto: Copp Clark, 1966. Toronto: University of Toronto Press, 1995.

1965    *Lament for a Nation: the Defeat of Canadian Nationalism.* Toronto: McClelland and Stewart, 1965, 1970. Ottawa: Carleton University Press, 1994. Montreal, Kingston: McGill–Queen's University Press, 1995.

1966    "A Critique of the New Left," *Canada and Radical Social Change.* Montreal: Black Rose, 1966, 55–61.

1969    *Technology and Empire: Perspectives on North America.* Toronto: House of Anansi Press, 1969.

1971    *Time as History.* Toronto: University of Toronto Press, 1971, 1995.

1978    *English-Speaking Justice.* Sackville, NB: Mount Allison University, 1978. Toronto: Anansi Press and Notre Dame: Notre Dame Press, 1985. Toronto: Anansi Press, 1998.

1983    "Introduction," Bithika Mukerji, *Neo-Vedanta and Modernity: Toward an Understanding of the Ontology of Bliss in the Context of Modernity.* Varanasi: Ashutosh Prakashan Sansthan, 1983.

1986    "The Moving Image of Eternity," *Ideas.* Toronto: CBC, 1986.

1986    *Technology and Justice.* Toronto: House of Anansi Press, 1986.

1990    "Two Theological Languages." In Whillier, *Two Theological Languages*, 8–19.

2006    "Five Lectures on Christianity." In Angus, Dart, and Peters, *Athens and Jerusalem*, 2006, 227–37.

**Collections**

Christian, William, and Sheila Grant, eds. *The George Grant Reader.* Toronto, Canada: University of Toronto Press, 1998.

Christian, William, ed. *George Grant: Selected Letters edited, with an introduction by William Christian*. Toronto: University of Toronto Press, 1996.

Davis, Arthur, and Peter C. Emberley, eds. *Collected Works of George Grant*: *Volume 1 (1933–1950)*. Toronto: University of Toronto Press, 2000.

Davis, Arthur, ed. *Collected Works of George Grant*: *Volume 2 (1951–1959)*. Toronto: University of Toronto Press, 2002.

Davis, Arthur, and Henry Roper, eds. *Collected Works of George Grant*: *Volume 3 (1960–1969)*. Toronto: University of Toronto Press, 2005.

Davis Arthur, and Henry Roper, eds. *Collected Works of George Grant*: *Volume 4: (1970?1988)*. Toronto: University of Toronto Press, 2009.

**Interviews**

Cayley, David. *George Grant in Conversation*. Toronto: Anansi, 1995.

———. "The Moving Image of Eternity." CBC *Ideas* Series, Part III. Canadian Broadcasting Corporation. Feb. 10, 1986. Transcript.

Christian, William, ed. "George Grant and Religion: A Conversation Prepared and Edited by William Christian." *Journal of Canadian Studies* 26.1 (1991) 42–63.

Schmidt, Larry, ed. *George Grant in Process*. Toronto: Anansi, 1978.

## George Grant: Secondary Sources

Angus, Ian, Ronald Dart, and Randy Peg Peters, eds. *Athens and Jerusalem: George Grant's Theology, Philosophy, and Politics*. University of Toronto Press, 2006.

Angus, Ian. "Athens and Jerusalem? A Critique of the Relationship between Philosophy and Religion in George Grant's Thought." *Journal of Canadian Studies* 39.2 (Spring 2005) 1–24.

Anderson, Fulton H. "Introduction." In J. A. Irving, *Philosophy in Canada: A Symposium*. Toronto: University of Toronto Press, 1952.

Arapura, John G. "Modern Thought and the Transcendent: Some observations based on an Eastern View." In Combs, *Modernity and Responsibility*, 51–61.

Athanasiadis, H. *George Grant and the Theology of the Cross*. Toronto: University of Toronto Press, 2001.

———. "Waiting at the Foot of the Cross: The Spirituality of George Grant." In Angus, Dart, and Peters, *Athens and Jerusalem*, 256–69.

Badertscher, J. "George P. Grant and Jacques Ellul on freedom in technological society." In Schmidt, *George Grant in Process*, 79–89.

Barua, Arati. *Gandhi and Grant: Their Philosophical Affinities*. New Delhi: Northern Book Centre, 2010.

Beiner, Ronald. "Grant, Nietzsche, and Post-Christian Theism." In Davis, *George Grant and the Subversion of Modernity*, 109–38.

Bissell. *The Imperial Canadian: Vincent Massey in Office.* Toronto: University of Toronto, 1986.

Blodgett, E. D. "George Grant, the Uncertain Nation and Diversity of Being." *Canadian Literature* 152/153 (Spring/Summer 1997) 107–23.

Bradshaw, Leah. "Love and Will in the Miracle of Birth: An Arendtian Critique of George Grant on Abortion." In Davis, *George Grant and the Subversion of Modernity*, 220–39.

Bryant, M. Darrol. "The Barren Twilight: History and Faith in Grant's Lament." In Schmidt, *George Grant in Process,* 110–19.

Christian, William. "Behind Every Great Man …" *History Wire* (Dec. 16, 2009). <http://www.historywire.ca/en/post/20509>. Accessed Jan. 10, 2010.

———. *George Grant: A Biography*. Toronto: University of Toronto Press, 1994.

———. "George Grant: Introduction to His Life and Philosophy." In Barua, *Gandhi and Grant*, 2010, 1–11.

———. "George Grant and Love: A Comment on Ian Box's 'George Grant and the Embrace of Technology.'" *Canadian Journal of Political Science / Revue canadienne de science politique* 16.2 (June/juin 1983) 349–54.

———. "George Grant and the Terrifying Darkness." In Schmidt, *George Grant in Process,* 167–78.

———. "Grant, George Parkin," *The Canadian Encyclopedia* (2012). <http://www.thecanadianencyclopedia.com/articles/george–grant>.

———. "Waiting for Grace: Philosophy and Politics in Plato's *Republic*." *Canadian Journal of Political Science / Revue canadienne de science politique* 21.1 (March/mars 1988) 57–82.

Cooper, Barry. "George Grant and the Revival of Political Philosophy." In Emberley, *By Loving Our Own*, 97–122.

Dart, Ronald S. *The Canadian Red Tory Tradition: Ancient Roots, New Routes*. Dewdney: Synaxis Press, 1999.

———. "Michael Ignatieff, George Grant, and India," CICS Report 4:3 (Aug. 2009) 6.

———. "Political Ressourcement: Anabaptist Inaccuracies, Radical Orthodoxy, Red Toryism and George Grant." *The Owl: George Grant Journal* (Oct. 16, 2010). <http://www.theowlgeorgegrant.blogspot.ca/2010/10/political-ressourcement-anabaptist.html>.

———. "Review, *Lament for a Nation*." *Clarion Journal of Spirituality and Justice* (Jan. 2006). <http://www.clarion–journal.com/clarion_journal_of_spirit/ 2006/06/george_grant_la.html>.

———. *Spiders and Bees: Collected Essays by Ronald S. Dart*. Abbotsford: Fresh Wind Press, 2008.

Dart, Ronald S., and Brad Jersak.*George P. Grant: Canada's Lone Wolf*. Abbotsford: Fresh Wind Press, 2011.

Davis, Arthur, ed. *George Grant and the Subversion of Modernity*. Toronto: University of Toronto Press, 1996.

Emberley, Peter C., ed. *By Loving Our Own: George Grant and the Legacy of Lament for a Nation*. Ottawa: Carleton University Press, 1990.

———. "George Parkin Grant: A Bibliographical Introduction." In Schmidt, *George Grant in Process*, 195–9.

Flewwelling, Martin. "Profile: George Grant." Atlantic Advocate 12 (1987) 5.

Flinn, Frank K. "George Grant's Critique of Technological Liberalism." Doctoral thesis. St. Michael's College, University of Toronto, 1981.

Forbes, Hugh Donald. *George Grant: A Guide to His Thought*. Toronto: University of Toronto Press, 2007.

Gillespie, Michael Allen. "George Grant and the Tradition of Political Philosophy." In Emberley, *By Loving Our Own*, 123–31.

Graham, Nita. "Teaching Against the Spirit of the Age: George Grant and Museum Culture." In Davis, *George Grant and the Subversion of Modernity*, 285–303.

Grant, Sheila. "Afterword." In Grant, *Lament for a Nation*, 97–9.

———. "George Grant and the Theology of the Cross." In Davis, *George Grant and the Subversion of Modernity*, 243–62.

Greenspan, Louis. "The Unravelling of Liberalism." In Davis, *George Grant and the Subversion of Modernity*, 201–19.

Hanly, Charles, ed. *Revolution and Response: Selections from the Toronto International Teach–in.* Toronto/Montreal: McClelland and Stewart Ltd., 1966.

Hall, Douglas John. "The Significance of Grant's Cultural Analysis for Christian Theology in North America," In Schmidt, *George Grant in Process*, 120–9.

———. *Thinking the Faith: Christian Theology in North American Context*. Minneapolis: Fortress Press, 1991.

Havers, Grant. "George Grant and Leo Strauss: Modernist and Postmodernist Conservatisms." *Topia* 8 (Fall 2002) 91–106.

———. "Leo Strauss's Influence on George Grant." In Angus, Dart and Peters, *Athens and Jerusalem*, 2006, 124–35.

Heaven, Edwin B., and David R. Heaven. "Some Influences of Simone Weil on George Grant's Silence." In Schmidt, *George Grant in Process*, 68–78.

Heaven, Ted. "George Grant on Socrates and Christ." In Angus, Dart, and Peters, *Athens and Jerusalem*, 300–22.

Heyking, John Von, and Barry Cooper. "'A Cow is Just a Cow': George Grant and Eric Voegelin on the United States." In Angus, Dart, and Peters, *Athens and Jerusalem*, 166–89.

Ignatieff, Michael. *True Patriot Love: Four Generations in Search of Canada.* Toronto, ON: Penguin Group Canada, 2009.

Jersak, Brad. *Minerva's Snowy Owl: Essays in Political Theology.* Abbotsford: Fresh Wind Press, 2012.

———. *We Are Not Our Own: The Platonic Christianity of George P. Grant: From the Cave to the Cross and Back Again with Simone Weil.* Doctoral Thesis, Bangor University Wales, 2012.

Kaethler, Andrew. *The Synthesis of Athens and Jerusalem: George Grant's Defense Against Modernity.* Berlin, Leipzig: VDM, 2009.

Lampert, Laurence. "The Uses of Philosophy in George Grant." In Schmidt, *George Grant in Process,* 179–94.

Lathangue, Robin. "In Search of the True George Grant." *Sophia* 43.2 (Oct. 2004) 119–23.

Lee, Dennis. "Grant's Impasse." In Emberley, *By Loving Our Own*, 11–39.

Matthews, Robin. *George Grant's Betrayal of Canadian Nationalism*. Vancouver: Northlands Publications, 2004.

———. "Nationalism, Technology, and Canadian Survival." *Journal of Canadian Studies* 5.4 (1970) 44–9.

McCarroll, Pam. "The Whole as Love." In Angus, Dart, and Peters, *Athens and Jerusalem*, 270–86.

Mendelson, Alan. *Exiles from Nowhere: The Jews and the Canadian Elite*. Montreal: Robin Brass Studio, 2008.

Nickelson, Graeme. "Freedom and the Good." In Angus, Dart, and Peters, *Athens and Jerusalem*, 323–40.

O'Donovan, Joan E. *George Grant and the Twilight of Justice*. Toronto: University of Toronto Press, 1984.

Peters, Randy Pegg. "Three Wise Men from the East: Eastern Orthodox Influences on George Grant." In Angus, Dart, and Peters, *Athens and Jerusalem*, 238–55.

Potter, Andrew. "Introduction to the 40th Anniversary Edition." In Grant, *Lament for a Nation*, ix–lxviii.

Schmidt, Larry, ed. *George Grant in Process: Essays and Conversations*. Toronto: House of Anansi Press, 1978.

———. "George Grant on Simone Weil as Saint and Thinker." In Davis, *George Grant and the Subversion of Modernity*, 263–84.

Sheppard, W. R. "The Suffering of Love: George Grant and Simone Weil." In Whillier, *Two Theological Languages,* 20–62.

Sibley, Robert C. *Northern Spirits: John Watson, George Grant, and Charles Taylor—Appropriations of Hegelian Political Thought*. Montreal and Kingston, London, Ithica: McGill–Queens University Press, 2008.

Slater, John G., ed. *Minerva's Aviary: Philosophy at Toronto 1843–2003*. Toronto/Buffalo/London: University of Toronto Press, 2005.

Taylor, Charles. *Radical Tories*. Toronto: House of Anansi, 1982.

Tovell, Vincent, prod. *The Owl and the Dynamo: The Vision of George Grant*. Canadian Broadcasting Corporation, 1980.

Ward, Bruce. "George Grant and the Problem of Theodicy in Western Christianity." In Whillier, *Two Theological Languages,* 94–104.

Whillier, Wayne, ed. *Two Theological Languages by George Grant and Other Essays in Honour of His Work*. Toronto Studies of Theology. Vol. 43. Lewiston/Queenston/Lampeter: Mellen, 1990.

Woodcock, George. "Review of Joan E. O'Donovan's *George Grant and the Twilight of Justice*," *The Globe and Mail* (Feb. 16, 1985).

Zylstra, Bernard. "Philosophy, Revelation and Modernity: Crossroads in the Thought of George Grant." In Schmidt, *George Grant in Process*, 148–56.

## Simone Weil: Primary Sources (English)

Weil, Simone. *First and Last Notebooks*. Trans. Richard Rees. London, New York, Toronto: Oxford University Press, 1970.

———. *Formative Writings*, 1929–1941. Trans. D.T. McFarland and W. Van Ness. Amherst: University of Massachusetts, 1987.

———. *Gateway to God.* David Raper, ed. London: Fontana, 1974.

———. *Gravity and Grace.* Trans. Emma Craufurd and Mario von dur Ruhr. London/New York: Routledge, 1952, 2002.

———. *Intimations of Christianity Among the Ancient Greeks.* Trans. Elisabeth Chas Geissbuhler. London, New York: Ark, 1957, 1987.

———. *Lectures on Philosophy.* Trans. Hugh Price. Cambridge: Cambridge University Press, 1959, 1978.

———. *Letter to a Priest.* Trans. A. F. Wills. New York: Penguin, 1954, 2003.

———. *The Need for Roots: Prelude to a Declaration of Duties towards Mankind.* Trans. A. F. Wills. New York and London: Routledge, 1952.

———. *The Notebooks.* Trans. Arthur Wills. 2 Vols. London: Routledge and Kegan Paul, 1956.

———. *On Science, Necessity, and the Love of God.* Trans. Richard Rees. London, New York, Toronto: Oxford University Press, 1968.

———. *Oppression and Liberty*. Trans. Arthur Wills and John Petrie. Amherst, MS: University of Massechusetts Press, 1973.

———. *Simone Weil Reader.* George A. Panichas, ed. Mt. Kisco, NY: Moyer Bell, Ltd., 1977.

———. *Simone Weil: Selected Essays, 1934–43.* Trans. by Richard Rees. London: Oxford University Press, 1962.

———. *Simone Weil: Seventy Letters.* Trans. by Richard Rees. London: Oxford University Press, 1965.

———. *Simone Weil: Writings Selected with an Introduction by Eric O. Springsted.* Modern Spiritual Masters Series. Maryknoll, NY: Orbis Books, 1998.

———. *Thinking God: A Bilingual Simone Weil Reader*. Trans. Benjamin Bergery. 2002–05. <http://simoneweil.net/lesautres.htm>.

———. *Waiting for God*. Trans. Emma Craufurd. New York: Harper, 1951, 2009.

### Simone Weil: Primary Sources (French)

———. *Attente de Dieu [Lettres écrites du 19 janvier au 26 mai 1942]*. Éditions Fayard, 1966.

———. *La Connaissance surnaturelle*. Paris: Gallimard, 1950.

———. *La Source grecque*. Paris: Gallimard, 1963.

———. *Écrits historiques et politiques*. Œuvres completes Tome II. Vol. 1. Éditions Gallimard, 1988.

———. *Écrits de Londres et dernières letters*. Paris: Gallimard, 1957.

———. Intuitions pré–chrétiennes. Nouvelle edition. Paris: Fayard, 1985.

———. *La pesanteur et la grace*. Librairie Plon, 1947.

———. *Lettre* à un religeiux. Éditions Gallimard, 1951.

———. *Oeuvres*, Quarto Gallimard, 1999.

———. *Pensées sans ordre concernant l'amour de Dieu*. Paris: Gallimard, 1968.

### Simone Weil: Secondary Sources

Bauer, J. Edgar. "Simone Weil: Kenotic Thought and 'Sainteté Nouvelle.'" *Center for Studies on New Religions Conference*. Salt Lake City and Provo, Utah (June 20–23, 2002). <http://www.cesnur.org/2002/slc/bauer.htm#_ednref30>.

Bell, Richard H. *Simone Weil: The Way of Justice as Compassion*. Lanham: Rowman and Littlefield Publishers, 1998.

Courtine–Denamy, Sylvie. *Three Women in Dark Times: Edith Stein, Hannah Arendt, Simone Weil, or Amor Fati, Amor Mundi*. Trans. G.M. Goshgarian. Ithaca: Cornell University Press, 2000.

De Lussy, Florence. "To On: A Nameless Something over Which the Mind Stumbles." In Doering and Springsted, *The Christian Platonism of Simone Weil*, 115–32.

Doering, E. Jane, and Eric O. Springsted, eds. *The Christian Platonism of Simone Weil*. Notre Dame: University of Notre Dame Press, 2004.

Doering E. Jane. *Simone Weil and the Specter of Self–Perpetuating Force.* Notre Dame, IN: University of Notre Dame Press, 2010.

Gabellieri, Emmanuel. "Reconstructing Platonism: The Trinitarian Metaxology of Simone Weil." In Doering and Springsted, *The Christian Platonism of Simone Weil*, 133–58.

Giniewski, Paul. *Simone Weil: Ou, La haine de soi.* Paris: Berg Intl., 1978.

George, Jim. "Leo Strauss, Neoconservatism and US Foreign Policy: Esoteric Nihilism and the Bush Doctrine." *International Politics* 42.2 (2005), 174–202.

Gray, Francine du Plessix. "Loving and Hating Simone Weil." *The American Scholar* 70.3 (Summer 2001): 5–11.

———. *Simone Weil.* New York: Viking, 2001.

Little, J. P. *Simone Weil: Waiting on Truth.* Oxford: St. Martin's Press, 1988.

Mackenzie, Rod. "Education and the Journey of the Soul: From Paranoia to Metanoia." <http://www.philosophy–of–education.org/pdfs/Saturday/Mackenzie.pdf>.

Nava, Alexander. *The Mystical and Prophetic Thought of Simone Weil and Gustavo Gutiérrez: Reflections on the Mystery and Hiddenness of God.* Albany: State University of New York Press, 2001.

Nevin, Thomas R. *Simone Weil: Portrait of a Self–exiled Jew.* Chapel Hill: University of North Carolina Press, 1991.

Perrin, Joseph Marie, and Gustave Thibon. *Simone Weil as We Knew Her.* Trans. Emma Craufurd. London: Routledge, 2003.

Pétrement, Simone. *Simone Weil: A Life.* Trans. Raymond Rosenthal. New York: Pantheon Books, 1976.

Ross, Michael. "Transcendence, Immanence, and Practical Deliberation." In Doering and Springsted, *The Christian Platonism of Simone Weil*, 43–60.

Schmidt, Larry, and Patrick Patterson, "The Christian Materialism of Simone Weil." In Doering and Springsted, *The Christian Platonism of Simone Weil*, 77–94.

Sheppard, W. R. "The Suffering of Love: George Grant and Simone Weil." Whillier, *Two Theological Languages*, 20–62.

Springsted, Eric O. "The Attention of Awaiting God." *Paying Attention to the Sky* (June 9, 2010). <http://payingattentiontothesky.com/category/simone–weil–2/>.

———. *Christus Mediator: Platonic Mediation in the Thought of Simone Weil*. Chico: Scholars Press, 1983.

———. "Contradiction, Mystery, and the Use of Words in Simone Weil." *Paying Attention to the Sky* (June 9, 2010). <http://payingattentiontothesky.com/2010/06/09/contradiction–mystery–and–the–use–of–words–in–simone–weil——eric–o–springsted/>.

———. "I Dreamed I Saw St. Augustine …" In Doering and Springsted, *The Christian Platonism of Simone Weil*, 209–28.

Taubes, Susan A. "The Absent God." *Journal of Religion* 35 (Jan. 1995) 6–16.

Vetö, Miklós. *The Religious Metaphysics of Simone Weil*. Trans. Joan Dargan. Albany: State University of New York Press, 1994.

**Other Sources Consulted**

Adamson, John. "Oliver Cromwell and the Long Parliament." In John Morrill, ed. *Oliver Cromwell and the English Revolution*. London: Longman, 1990, 76–84.

Adorno, Theodor. *Negative Dialectics* (1966). Trans. E. B. Ashton. New York, NY: Seabury Press, 1973.

Alcoholics Anonymous. The Big Book Online. Fourth Edition. A. A. World Services, Inc., 2006. <http://www.aa.org/bigbookonline/>.

Anderson, John M. "Introduction." In Heidegger, *Discourse on Thinking*, 11–39.

Aquinas, Thomas. *The Summa Theologica of St. Thomas Aquinas*. Second and Revised Edition, 1920. Trans. Fathers of the English Dominican Province. <http://www.newadvent.org/summa/2001.htm>.

Arendt, Hannah. *The Human Condition*. Chicago, London: University of Chicago Press, 1958.

Armour, Leslie, and Elizabeth Trott. *The Faces of Reason: Philosophy in English Canada, 1850–1950,* (Waterloo: Wilfrid Laurier Press, 1981).

Asmis, Elizabeth. "Myth and Philosophy in Cleanthes' *Hymn to Zeus*," *Greek, Roman, and Byzantine Studies* 47 (2007) 413–29.

Augustine of Hippo. *Confessions of Saint Augustine*. Minneapolis: Filiquarian Pub. LLC, 2008.

Autenrieth, Georg. *A Homeric Dictionary for Schools and Colleges*. New York. Harper and Brothers, 1891. <http://www.perseus.tufts.edu>.

# Bibliography

Bacon, Francis. *The Advancement of Learning*. Public Domain Books, Apr 01, 2004. (Kindle Edition).

———. "The Masculine Birth of Time." In Benjamin Farrington, ed. *The Philosophy of Francis Bacon*. Chicago: Univ. of Chicago Press, 1964, 60–72. <http://isnature.org/files/Bacon_Masculine_Birth_of_Time.htm>.

Baillie, John. *Our Knowledge of God*. London: Oxford University Press, 1941.

Baroud, Ramzy. *My Father Was a Freedom Fighter: Gaza's Untold Story*. New York: Pluto Books, 2010.

Barry, William. "John Henry Newman." *The Catholic Encyclopedia*. Vol. 10. New York: Robert Appleton Company, 1911. <http://www.newadvent.org/cathen/10794a.htm>.

Benardete, Seth, ed. *Leo Strauss on Plato's Symposium*. Chicago, London: University of Chicago Press, 2001.

Benedict XVI. *Jesus of Nazareth*. Trans. Adrian J. Walker. New York: Doubleday, 2007.

———. "Three Stages in the Program of De–Hellenization." *Papal Address at the University of Regensburg* (Sept. 12, 2006). <http://www.crossroadsinitiative.com/library_article/981/De_Hellenization_Benedict_XVI.html>.

Blond, Phillip, ed. *Post–secular Philosophy: Between Philosophy and Theology*. London, New York: Routledge, 1998.

———. *Red Tory: How Left and Right Have Broken Britain and How We Can Fix It*. London: Faber and Faber, 2010.

Bloom, Allan. "Justice: John Rawls versus the Tradition of Political Philosophy." *Giants and Dwarfs: Essays 1960–1990*. New York: Simon and Schuster, 1990, 315–45.

Brothen, Tanya. "Obama Gives Second Annual Back–to–school Speech." *Obama Today* (Sept. 16, 2010). <http://blogs.america.gov/obama/2010/09/16/obama–gives–second–annual–back–to–school–speech/>.

Buber, Martin. *I and Thou*. London: T and T Clark, 1937.

Bultmann, Rudolph. *Theology of the New Testament*. New York: Charles Scribner's Sons, 1951. Waco, TX: Baylor University Press, 2007.

Calvin, John. *Institutes of the Christian Religion*, 2 vols. Trans. John Allen. Philadelphia, PA: Westminster, 1844.

Caputo, John D. *Heidegger and Aquinas: An Essay on Overcoming Metaphysics*. Bronx, NY: Fordham University Press, 1982.

———. *The Mystical Element in Heidegger's Thought.* Bronx, NY: Fordham University Press, 1986.

Carroll, James. *Jerusalem, Jerusalem: How the Ancient City Ignited Our Modern World.* New York, NY: Houghton Mifflin Harcourt Pub. Co., 2011.

Christian, William. *Parkin: Canada's Most Famous Forgotten Man.* Toronto: Blue Butterfly Books Pub. Inc., 2008.

Cochrane, Charles Norris. *Christianity and Classical Culture: A Study of Thought and Action from Augustus to Augustine.* New York: Oxford University Press, 1957.

The Council for Peace and Security: Association of Experts of National Security in Israel. <http://www.peacee–security–council.org>.

Daniels, Brandy. "The Academy, the Polis, and the Resurgence of Religion: An Interview with Graham Ward." The Other Journal 12 (Sept. 30, 2008). <http://www.theotherjournal.com/article.php?id=439>.

Dart, Ron. *Robin Mathews: Crown Prince of Canadian Political Poets.* Dewdney: Synaxis Press, 2002.

Descartes, Rene. *Discourse on the Method of Rightly Conduction the Reason, and Seeking Truth in the Sciences.* Forgotten Books, 2008. <http://www.forgottenbooks.org>.

———. *Discourse on Method and the Meditations.* Trans. F. E. Sutcliffe. Harmondsworth, UK: Penguin, 1968.

———. *Meditations on First Philosophy.* EZreads Pub., Mar. 06, 2009 (Kindle Edition).

———. *Rules for the Direction of the Mind.* Trans. E.S. Haldane and G. R. T. Ross. Chicago: Encyclopaedia Britannica, 1971.

Despland, Michel. *The Education of Desire: Plato and the Philosophy of Religion.* Toronto, Buffalo, London: University of Toronto Press, 1985.

Ebeling, Gerhard. *Luther: An Introduction to His Thought.* London: Collins, 1970.

Farrer, Austin. *Love Almighty and Ills Unlimited.* Garden City, NY: Doubleday, 1961.

"The Gospel of Mary (BG 8502)." In James Robinson, ed. *The Nag Hammadi Library in English.* San Francisco: Harper and Row, 1981, 471–4.

Hankey, Wayne. "James Doull, Étienne Gilson and George Grant on Modernity and Platonism." *The Friend* 2.1 (2000) 18–21.

Hart, David B. "Christ and Nothing." *First Things* 136 (Oct. 2003) 47–55.

———. "Nihilism and Freedom: Is There a Difference?" *MacLaurin Campus Lectures* (Mar. 22, 2007). <http://www.marshillstudents.net/mp3s/david_bentley_hart_lecture.mp3>.

Hegel, Georg Wilhelm Friedrich. *Lectures on the Philosophy of World History.* Trans. H. B. Nisbet. New York, NY: Cambridge University Press, 1975.

———. *The Philosophy of History.* Trans. J. Sibree. Kitchner: Batoche Books, 2001.

Heidegger, Martin. *Discourse on Thinking: A Translation of Gelassenheit.* Trans. John M. Anderson and E. Hans Freund. New York: Harper and Row, 1966.

———. *Early Greek Thinking: The Dawn of Western Philosophy.* Trans. David Farrell Krell and Frank A. Capuzzi. San Francisco: Harper and Row, 1984.

———. *The Essence of Truth: On Plato's Cave Allegory and Theaetetus.* Trans. Ted Sadler. London: Continuum, 2002. Impact Edition, 2004.

———. *An Introduction to Metaphysics.* Trans. Ralph Manheim. New Haven, London: Yale University Press, 1959.

———. "The Question Concerning Technology." In Martin Heidegger, *The Question Concerning Technology, and Other Essays.* Trans. William Lovitt. New York: Harper and Row, 1977, 3–35. <http://www.wright.edu/cola/Dept/PHL/Class/P.Internet/PITexts/QCT.html>. Accessed Jan. 15, 2011.

———. *What is Called Thinking? A Translation of Was Heisst Denken?* Trans. J. Glenn Gray. New York, San Francisco, Hagerstown, London: Harper and Row, 1968.

Heraclitus. *Fragments: The Collected Wisdom of Heraclitus.* Trans. B. Haxton. New York: Viking, 2001.

Heschel, Abraham Joshua. *Moral Grandeur and Spiritual Audacity: Essays Edited by Susannah Heschel.* New York: Farrar, Straus and Giroux, 1996.

Hoffman, Tobias, ed. *Weakness of Will from Plato to Present.* Studies in Philosophy and History of Philosophy. Vol. 49. Washington, DC: CUA Press, 2008.

Hooker, Richard. *Of the Laws of Ecclesiastical Polity.* Book 1. R. W. Church, ed. Oxford: Clarendon Press, 1880.

Hopkins, Gerard Manley. *Poems*. London: Humphrey Milford, 1918; Bartleby.com, 1999. <www.bartleby.com/122/>.

Hotam, Yotam. "On Reason and Revelation: The Correspondence between Eric Voegelin and Leo Strauss." *Negotiating Jewish Knowledge – Transitions and Transformations*. Simon Dubnow Institute for Jewish History and Culture, Jerusalem (Nov. 2007). <http://hsf.bgu.ac.il/cjt/files/electures/Reason–Revelation–Voegelin–Strauss1.htm>.

Hume, David. *Dialogues Concerning Natural Religion*. Mobile Reference, Jan 9, 2009 (Kindle Edition).

———. *An Enquiry Concerning Human Understanding*. Public Domain Books, Jan. 1, 2006 (Kindle Edition).

Huskinson, Lucy. *Nietzsche and Jung: the Whole Self in the Union of Opposites*. New York: Brunner–Routledge, 2004.

Ignatieff, George. *The Making of a Peacemonger: The Memoirs of George Ignatieff*. Toronto: University of Toronto Press, 1985.

"Ions Overview," *Institute of Noetic Sciences* (2012). <http://www.noetic.org/about/overview/>.

Jahn, Detlev. "Conceptualizing Left and Right in Comparative Politics." *Party Politics* 17 (Nov. 2011) 745–65.

James, William. *The Varieties of Religious Experience*. Rockville, MD: Arc Manor, 2008.

Janssens, David. *Between Athens and Jerusalem: Philosophy, Prophecy, and Politics in Leo Strauss's Early Thought*. Albany, NY: State University of New York Press, 2008.

Kant, Immanuel. *Basic Writings of Kant*. Allen W. Wood, ed. New York: Modern Library, 2001.

———. "On the Failure of All Philosophical Theodicies." In Michael Despland. *Kant on History and Religion*. Montreal: McGill–Queen's University Press, 1973.

"Karites." *Theoi Greek Mythology*. Auckland: The Theoi Project, 2000–11. <http://www.theoi.com/Ouranios/Kharites.html>.

Leibniz, Gottfried Wilhem. *Philosophical Papers and Letters*. 2nd edition. Leroy E. Loemker, ed. Dordrecht: Reidel, 1958.

———. *Theodicy: Essays on the Goodness of God, the Freedom of Man, and the Origin of Evil*. New York, NY: Cosimo, Inc., 2009.

Lewis, C. S. *The Business of Heaven: Daily Readings from C. S. Lewis*. San Diego, New York, London: A Harvest Book, Harcourt Inc., 1984.

———. *The Discarded Image: An Introduction to Medieval and Renaissance Literature*. Cambridge: Cambridge University Press, 1964.

Lewis, Michael. *Boomerang: Travels in the New Third World.* New York, London: Norton and Company, 2011.

Louth, Andrew. *The Origins of the Christian Mystical Tradition*. Oxford: Clarendon Press, 1981.

Lucier, James P. "Pickstock Chooses Radical Orthodoxy." *BNET UK* (Jan 10, 2000). <http://findarticles.com/p/articles/mi_m1571/is_2_16/ai_58617328/>.

Lukes, Steven. "Epilogue: The Grand Dichotomy of the Twentieth Century." In T. Ball and R. Bellamy, eds. *The Cambridge History of Twentieth Century Political Thought*. Cambridge: Cambridge University Press, 2003. <http://sociology.fas.nyu.edu/docs/IO/244/cup.pdf>.

Luther, Martin. "Against the Robbing and Murdering Hordes of Peasants." In E. G. Rupp and Benjamin Drewery, eds. *Martin Luther: Documents of Modern History*. London: Edward Arnold, 1970, 121–6.

———. *Concerning Christian Liberty*. Trans. R. S. Grignon. *The Five-Foot Shelf of Books*. The Harvard Classics. Vol. 36. New York: P. F. Collier and Son, 1910, 353–97. <http://www.iclnet.org/pub/resources/text/wittenberg/luther/web/cclib–2.html>.

———. *Luther's Works*. Timothy Lull, ed. Philadelphia: Fortress Press, 1957.

———. *Martin Luther: Selections from His Writings*. John Dillenberger, ed. New York: Doubleday, 1961.

MacIntyre, Alasdair. *After Virtue*. London: Gerald Duckworth and Co. Ltd., 1985.

———. *Whose Justice? Which Rationality?* Notre Dame: University of Notre Dame Press, 1988.

Mannal, Andreas. *Wisdom Point: Plato–Divided Line*. <http://andreas-mannal.blogspot.com/>.

Marion, Jean-Luc. "Descartes and Onto-theology." Trans. B. Bergo. In Philip Blond, ed. *Post–Secular Philosophy*. London, New York: Routledge, 1998, 67–106.

Mathews, Robin. *This Time, This Place*. Edmonton: Alberta Poetry North Publication, 1965.

Milbank, John, Catherine Pickstock, Graham Ward, eds. *Radical Orthodoxy: A New Theology*. London: Routledge, 1999.

Mockridge, Charles Henry. "The Hon. and Right Rev. John Strachen." *The Bishops of the Church of England in Canada and Newfoundland*, Toronto: F. N. W. Brown: 1896, 78–93. <strachen.awardspace.com>.

Murry, John Middletone. *Fyodor Dostoevsky.* London: Martin Secker, 1923.

*NAC*. National Archives of Canada, Ottawa.

Nietzsche, Friedrich. *The Anti–Christ.* Trans. R. J. Hollingdale: Penguin, 1990.

———. *Assorted Opinions and Maxims.* Trans. R. J. Hollingdale. Cambridge University Press, 1996.

———. *Beyond Good and Evil*, Trans. R. J. Hollingdale. Harmondsworth: Penguin, 1990.

———. *The Birth of Tragedy out of the Spirit of Music*. Trans. Shaun Whiteside. London: Penguin, 1993.

———. *The Gay Science.* Trans. Walter Kaufmann. New York: Vintage, 1974.

———. *Hammer of the Gods.* Trans. Stephen Metcalf. London: Creation Books, 1995.

———. *The Will to Power*. Tran. Walter Kaufmann and R. J. Hollingdale. New York: Vintage, 1967.

———. *Thus Spake Zarathustra.* Trans. Thomas Common. Ware: Wordsworth, 1997.

Owen, Wilfred. *Poems.* Project Gutenberg EBook of Poems. Prod. Alan R. Light, Gary M. Johnson, and David Widger, 2008.

<http://www.gutenberg.org/1/0/3/1034/>

Pesic, Peter. "Wrestling with Proteus: Francis Bacon and the 'Torture' of Nature." *Isis* 90.1 (Mar. 1999) 81–94. <http://www.scribd.com/doc/19081995/Bacon–and–Torture–of–Nature>.

Peters, F. E. *Greek Philosophical Terms: A Historical Lexicon.* New York: New York University Press, London: University of London Press Ltd., 1967.

Pétrement, Simone. *A Separate God: The Origins and Teachings of Gnosticism*. Trans. Carol Harrison. San Francisco: Harper San Francisco, 1990.

———. *le Dieu séparé: les origins du gnosticisme.* Paris: Les Editions du Cerf, 1984.

*The Philokalia: The Complete Text.* Vol. 1. Compiled by St. Nikodimos of the Holy Mountain and St. Makerios of Corinth. Trans. and ed. G. E. H. Palmer, Philip Sherrard, Kallistos Ware. London/Boston: Faber and Faber, 1979.

Pickstock, Catherine. *After Writing: On the Liturgical Consummation of Philosophy.* Oxford: Blackwell Pub. Ltd., 1998.

Plato. "The Allegory of the Cave," *Republic*, 6.514a.2–517a.7. Trans. Thomas Sheehan. <http://www.stanford.edu/class/ihum40/cave.pdf>.

———. *Apology.* Plato in Twelve Volumes. Vol. 1. Trans. Harold North Fowler. Cambridge: Harvard University Press; London, William Heinemann Ltd., 1966.

———. *Dialogues of Plato.* Trans. Benjamin Jowatt. Justin D. Kaplan, ed. New York: Simon and Schuster, 1950.

———. *Five Great Dialogues.* Trans. B. Jowatt. L. R. Loomis, ed. Roslyn, NY: Walter J. Black, 1942.

———. *Gorgias.* Plato in Twelve Volumes. Vol. 3. Trans. W.R.M. Lamb. Cambridge: Harvard University Press; London: William Heinemann Ltd., 1967.

———. *Letters.* Plato in Twelve Volumes. Vol. 7. Trans. R.G. Bury. Cambridge: Harvard University Press; London: William Heinemann Ltd., 1966.

———. *Phaedrus.* Plato in Twelve Volumes. Vol. 9. Trans. Harold N. Fowler. Cambridge: Harvard University Press; London: William Heinemann Ltd., 1925.

———. *The Republic.* Trans. H. D. P. Lee. Harmondsworth: Penguin Classics, 1955.

———. *The Republic.* Plato in Twelve Volumes Vols. 5 and 6. Trans. Paul Shorey. Cambridge: Harvard University Press; London: William Heinemann Ltd., 1969. <http://www.perseus.tufts.edu/hopper/>.

———. *The Republic (Greek edition). Platonis Opera.* John Burnet, ed. Oxford University Press, 1903. <http://www.perseus.tufts.edu/hopper/>.

———. *Symposium.* Plato in Twelve Volumes. Vol. 9. Trans. Harold N. Fowler. Cambridge: Harvard University Press; London: William Heinemann Ltd., 1925. <http://www.perseus.tufts.edu/hopper/>.

———. *Theaetetus*. Plato in Twelve Volumes. Vol. 12. Trans. Harold N. Fowler. Cambridge: Harvard University Press; London: William Heinemann Ltd., 1921. <http://www.perseus.tufts.edu/hopper/>.

———. *Timeaus*. Plato in Twelve Volumes. Vol. 9. Trans. W.R.M. Lamb. Cambridge: Harvard University Press; London: William Heinemann Ltd. 1925. <http://www.perseus.tufts.edu/hopper/>.

Pollock, John. *Moody: The Biography*. Chicago: Moody, 1983.

Porro, Pasquale. "Henry of Ghent." In Edward N. Zalta, ed. *The Stanford Encyclopedia of Philosophy* (Fall 2008 Edition), <http://plato.stanford.edu/archives/fall2008/entries/henry–ghent/>)

Puhalo, Lazar. "*Nous:* the Concord of Gnosis, Theoria and Theosis." Unpublished paper. Dewdney: All Saints Orthodox Monastery, 2011.

*Rebuilding America's Defenses: Strategy, Forces and Resources for a New Century*. The Project for the New American Century (Sept. 2000). <http://www.newamericancentury.org/RebuildingAmericasDefenses.pdf>.

Rohr, Richard. "The Franciscan Opinion." In Brad Jersak and Michael Hardin, eds., *Stricken by God?: Nonviolent Identification and the Victory of Christ*. Grand Rapids, MI: Eerdmans, 2007.

Rousseau, Jean–Jacques. "Letter to Voltaire on Optimism." In Voltaire. *Candide and Related Texts*, 108–22.

———. *On the Social Contract*. Trans. Donald A. Cress. Indianapolis, Cambridge: Hacket, 1987.

Salles, Ricardo, ed. *God and Cosmos in Stoicism*. Oxford, New York: Oxford University Press, 2009.

Schumacher, E. F. *A Guide for the Perplexed*. New York, Hagerstown, San Francisco, London: Harper and Row Pub., 1977.

Smith, Huston. *Beyond the Post-Modern Mind*. New York: Crossroads Pub. Co., 1982.

Speakman, Porter, dir. "With God on Our Side." Rooftop Productions, 2010.

Strauss, Leo. *Gesammelte Schriften Bd. 2: Philosophie und Gesetz—frühe Schriften*. Heinrich Meier, ed. Stuttgart/Weimar: Verlag J. B. Metzler, 1996.

———. *Natural Right and History*. Chicago: University of Chicago Press, 1953.

———. *Philosophy and Law: Contributions to the Understanding of*

      *Maimonides and His Predecessors*. Trans. Eve Adler. Albany, NY: State University of New York, 1995.

———. *An Introduction to Political Philosophy: Ten Essays by Leo Strauss*. Expanded version of *Political Philosophy: Six Essays by Leo Strauss*, 1975. Hilail Gilden, ed. Detroit: Wayne State UP, 1989.

———. *What is Political Philosophy? And Other Studies*. Glencoe, IL: Free Press, 1959.

Swift, Jonathan. *The Battle of the Books*. Classics–Unbound, Sept. 6, 2009 (Kindle Edition).

Tertullian. *Prescription against Hereticks; and the Apologeticks of St. Theophilus Bishop of Antioch to Autolycus against the Malicious Calumniator of the Christian Religion*. Trans. Joseph Betty. Oxford, 1722. <http://www.tertullian.org/articles/betty_prae/betty_prae.htm>.

Ulfers, Friedrich, and Mark Daniel Cohen. "Nietzsche's *Amor Fati*: the Embracing of an Undecided Fate." *The Nietzsche Circle*, 2007. <http://www.nietzschecircle.com/essayArchive9.html>.

Upton, Jason. "Campfires and Masquarades." Key of David Ministries, 2012. UBP.

Uždavinys, Algis. *The Golden Chain: An Anthology of Pythagorean and Platonic Philosophy*. Bloomington, IN: World Wisdom Inc., 2004.

Voegelin, Eric. *History of Political Ideas, Vol. 2: The Middle Ages to Aquinas*. The Collected Works of Eric Voegelin, Vol. 20. Peter Von Sivers, ed. Columbia, MO: University of Missouri Press, 1977.

———. "Liberalism and Its History." *The Review of Politics* 36 (1974) 504–20.

———. *The New Politics of Science: An Introduction*. Chicago, London: University of Chicago Press, 1952, 1987.

———. Order and History. Vol. 1, Israel and Revelation. Baton Rouge: LSU Press, 1956).

Voltaire. *Candide and Related Texts*. Trans. David Wootton. Indianapolis: Hacket Pub. Co. Ltd, 2000.

———. "Preface to the 'Poem on the Lisbon Disaster' (1756)." In Voltaire. *Candide and Related Texts*, 95–98.

———. "Poem on the Lisbon Disaster or Examination of this Axiom 'All is Well,'" *Selected Poems by Voltaire*. Trans. Joseph McCabe. London: Watts and Co., 1911. <http://books.google.ca/books?id=QwFhZlucjK4C>.

———. "Tout es Bien." *Philosophical Dictionary* (1764). Trans. Theodore Besterman. London and New York: Penguin Books, 1972.

"Voluntarism (philosophy)," *Britannica Concise Encyclopedia.* <http://www.answers.com/topic/voluntarism>.

Wallace, David Foster. *Infinite Jest.* Hachette Book Group, 2009 (Kindle Edition).

Weber, Max. *The Protestant Ethic and the Spirit of Capitalism.* Trans. Talcott Parsons. London/New York. Routledge, 1992.

Wesley, John. "Serious thoughts occasioned by the earthquake at Lisbon to which is subjoin'd An account of all the late earthquakes there and in other places" (1756). Gale ECCO, Print Editions, 2010.

Wheelwright, Philip, ed. *The Presocratics.* London: Collier; New York: MacMillan, 1966.

Woolverton, Linda. *Screen Play: Alice in Wonderland.* Walt Disney Pictures, 2010. <http://en.wikiquote.org/wiki/Alice_in_Wonderland_(2010_film)>.

Wright, N. T. *Jesus and the Victory of God.* Minneapolis: Fortress Press, 1996.

www.ingramcontent.com/pod-product-compliance
Lightning Source LLC
LaVergne TN
LVHW051837080426
835512LV00018B/2927